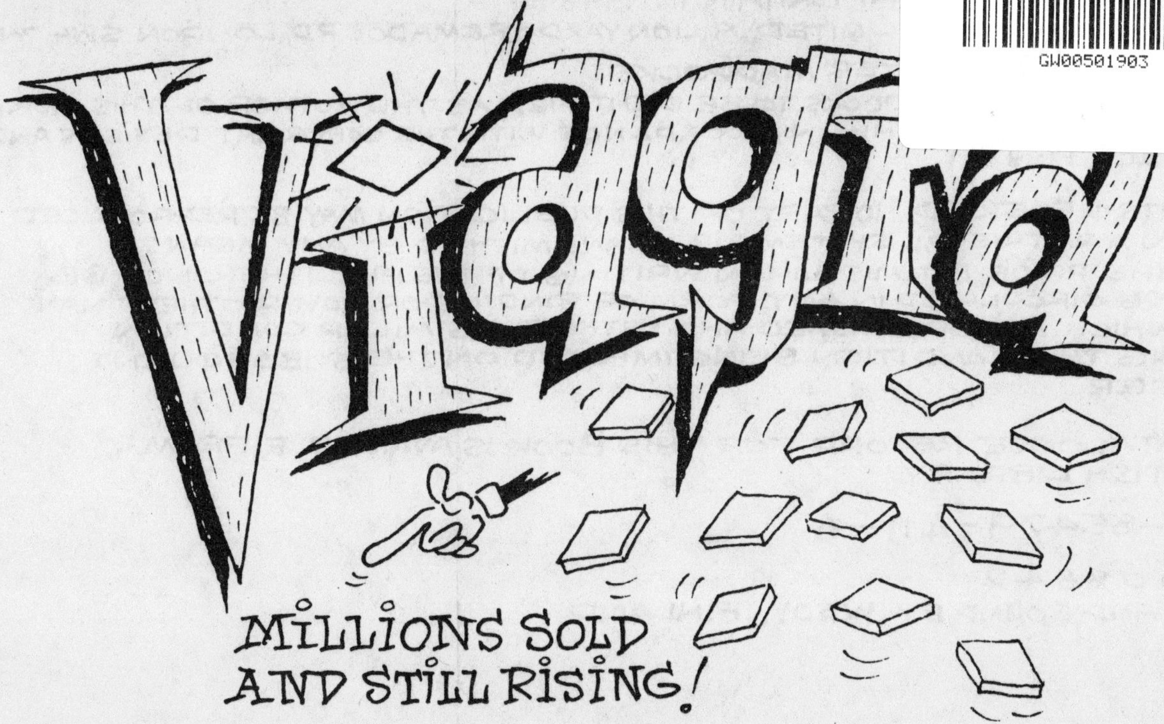
Viagra
MILLIONS SOLD
AND STILL RISING!

FIRST PUBLISHED IN GREAT BRITAIN IN 1998 BY
MICHAEL O'MARA BOOKS LIMITED. 9 LION YARD TREMADOC RD, LONDON. SW4 7NQ
VIAGRA ©1998 BY PETER MADDOCKS.

A CIP CATALOGUE RECORD FOR THIS BOOK IS AVAILABLE FROM
THE BRITISH LIBRARY.

ISBN/1-85479-411-6

1 3 5 7 9 10 8 6 4 2
PRINTED AND BOUND BY WSOY, FINLAND

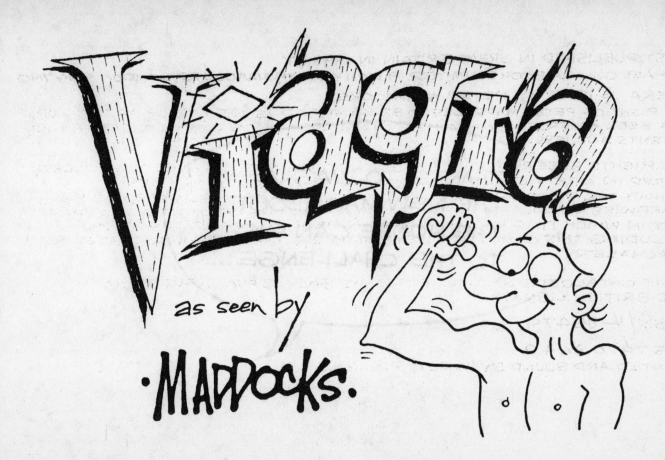

Viagra

as seen by

·MADDOCKS·

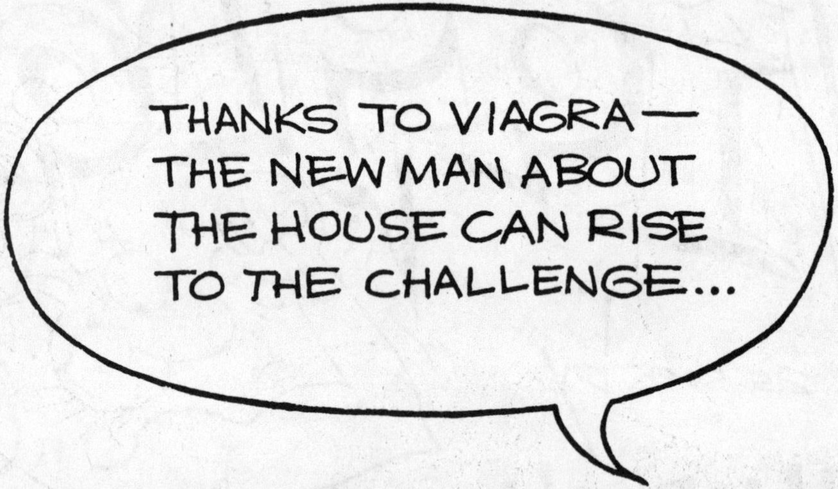
THANKS TO VIAGRA— THE NEW MAN ABOUT THE HOUSE CAN RISE TO THE CHALLENGE...

— POP IN A TABLET BEFORE RISING!

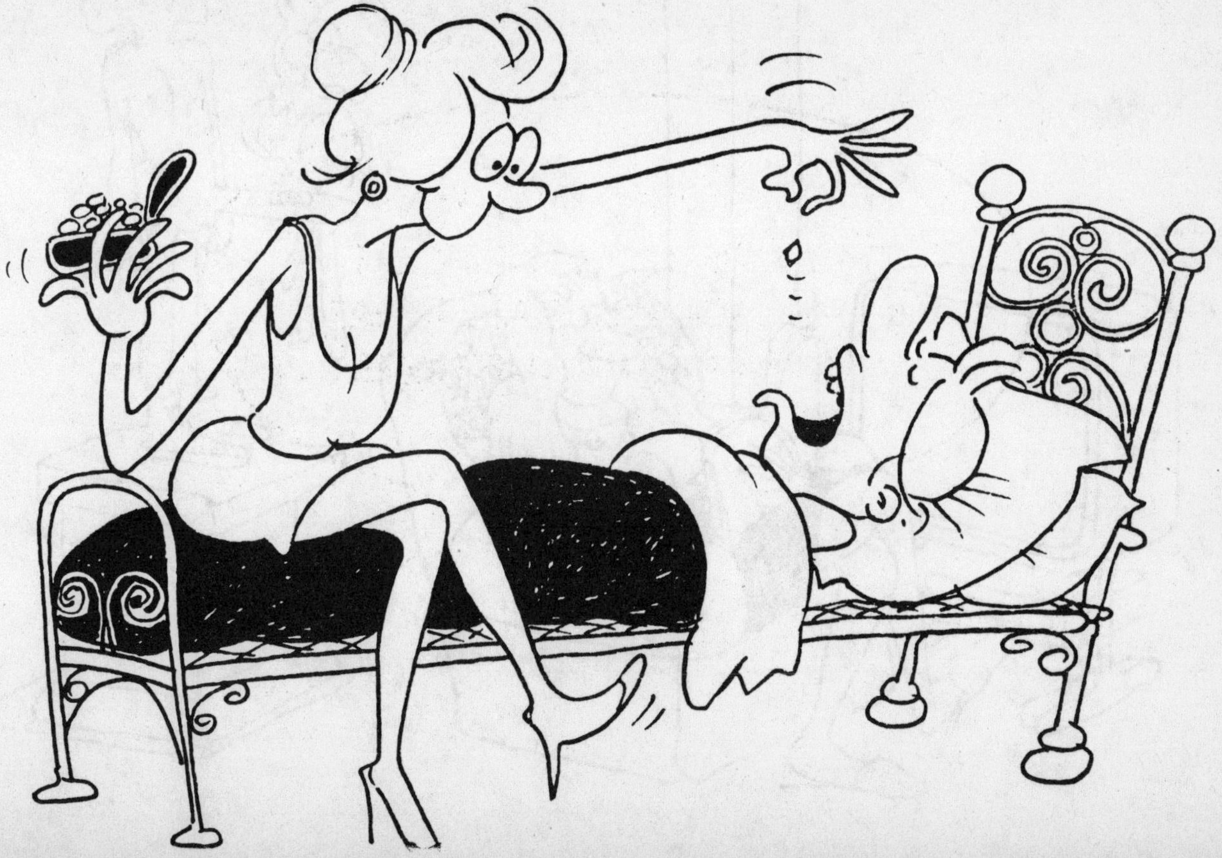

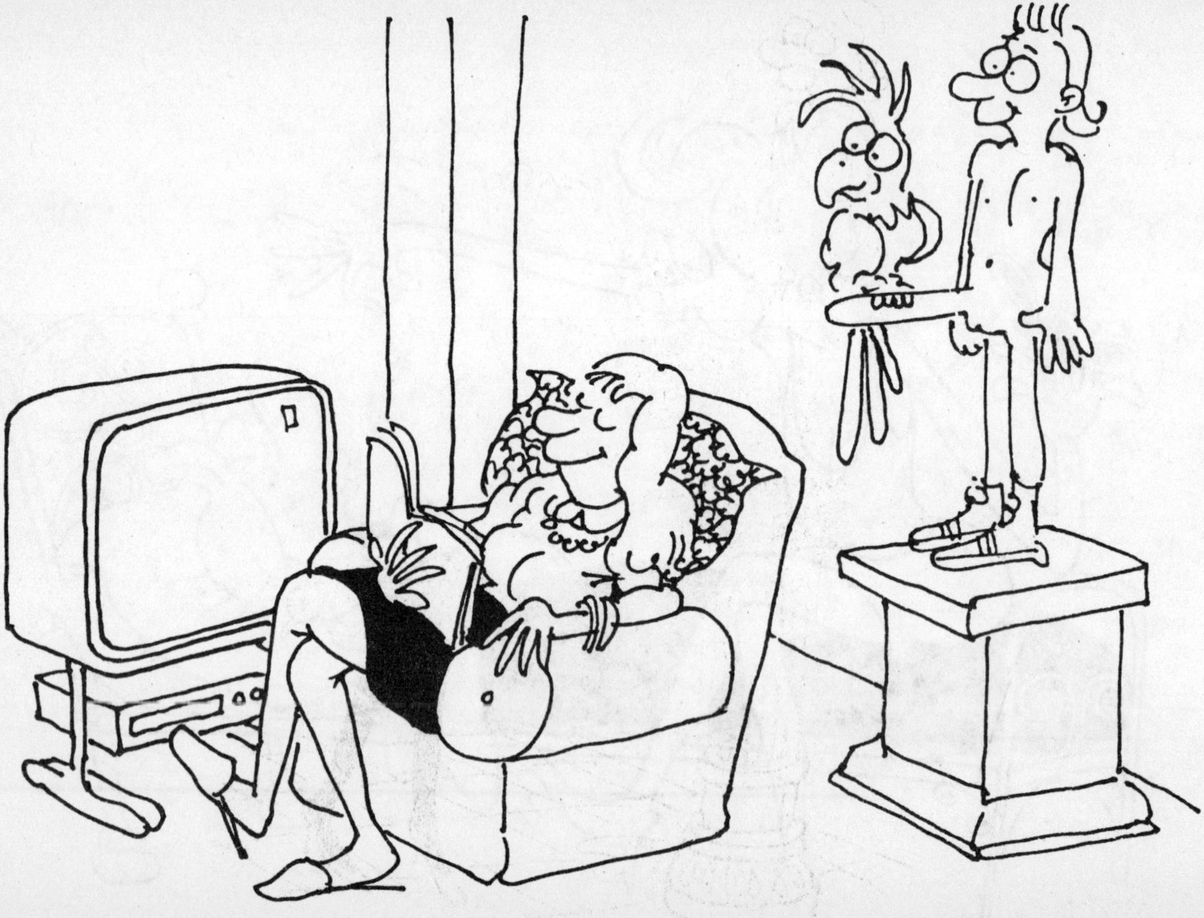

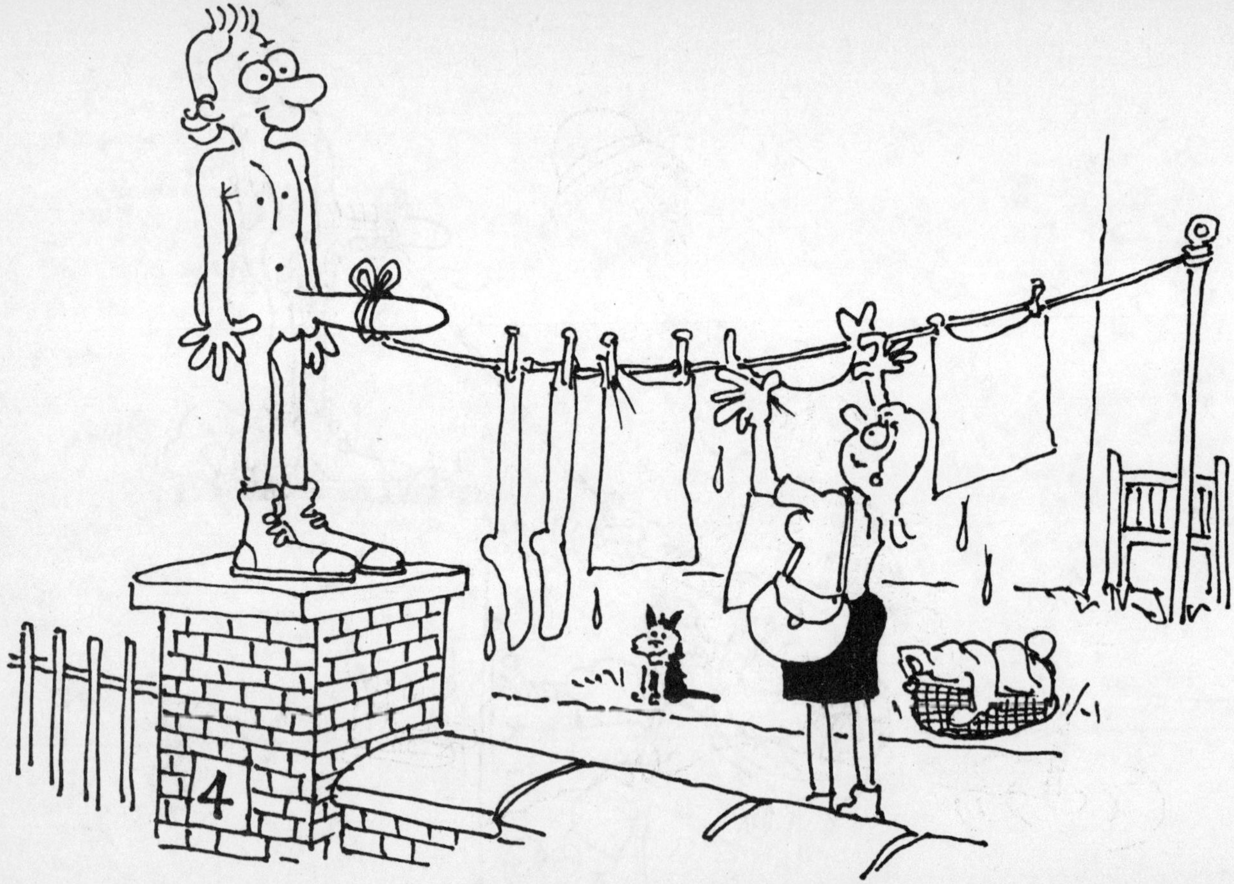
4

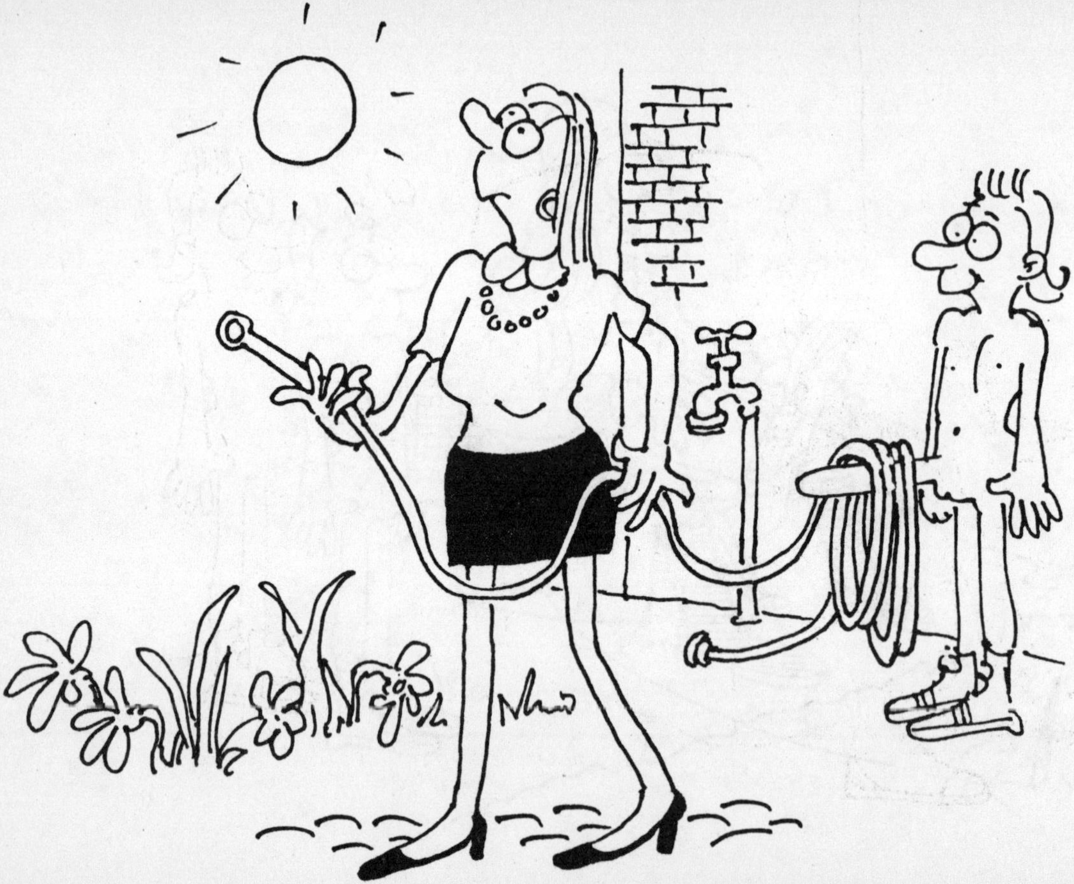

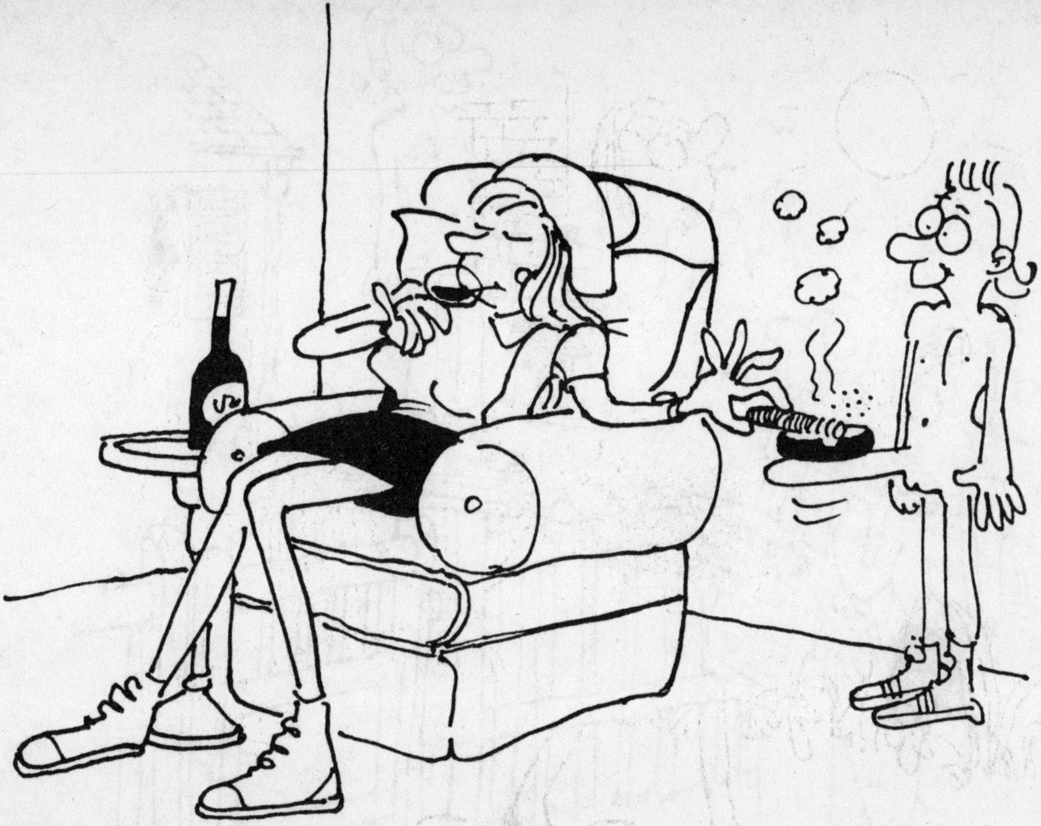

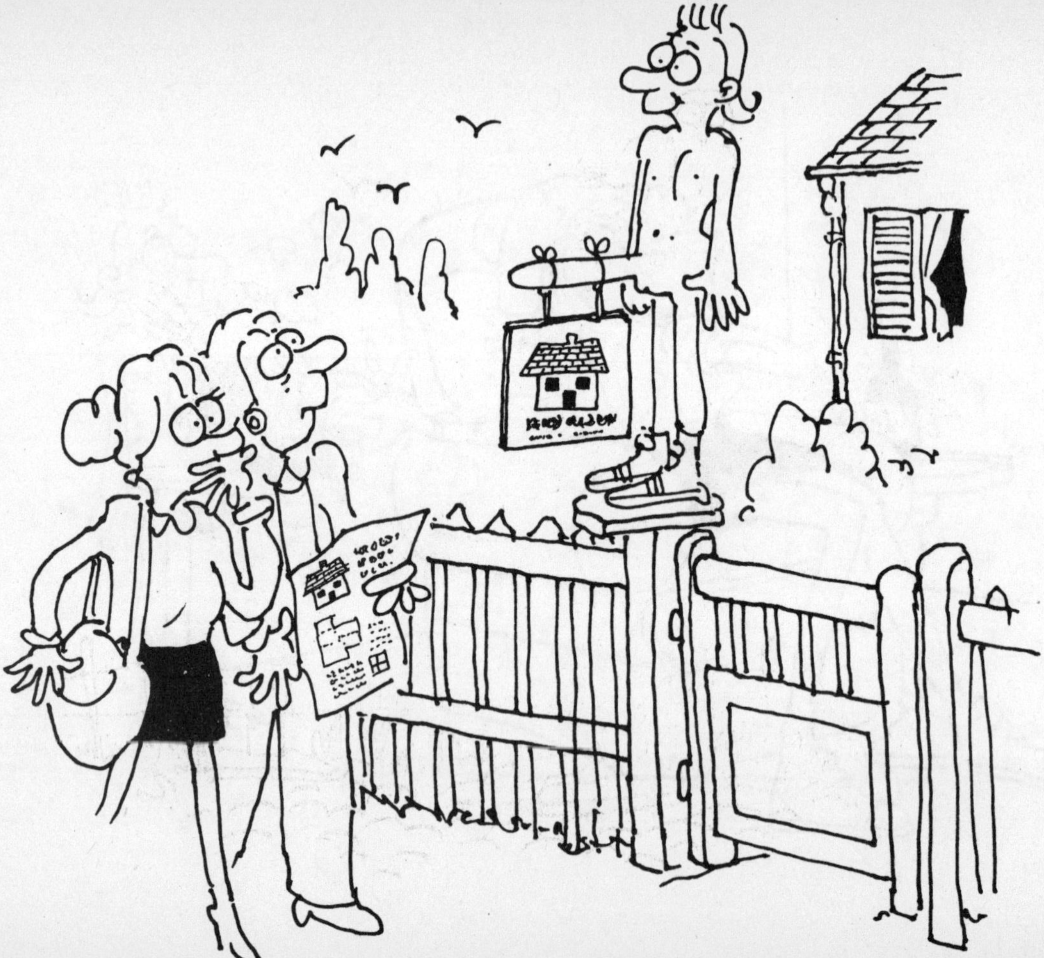

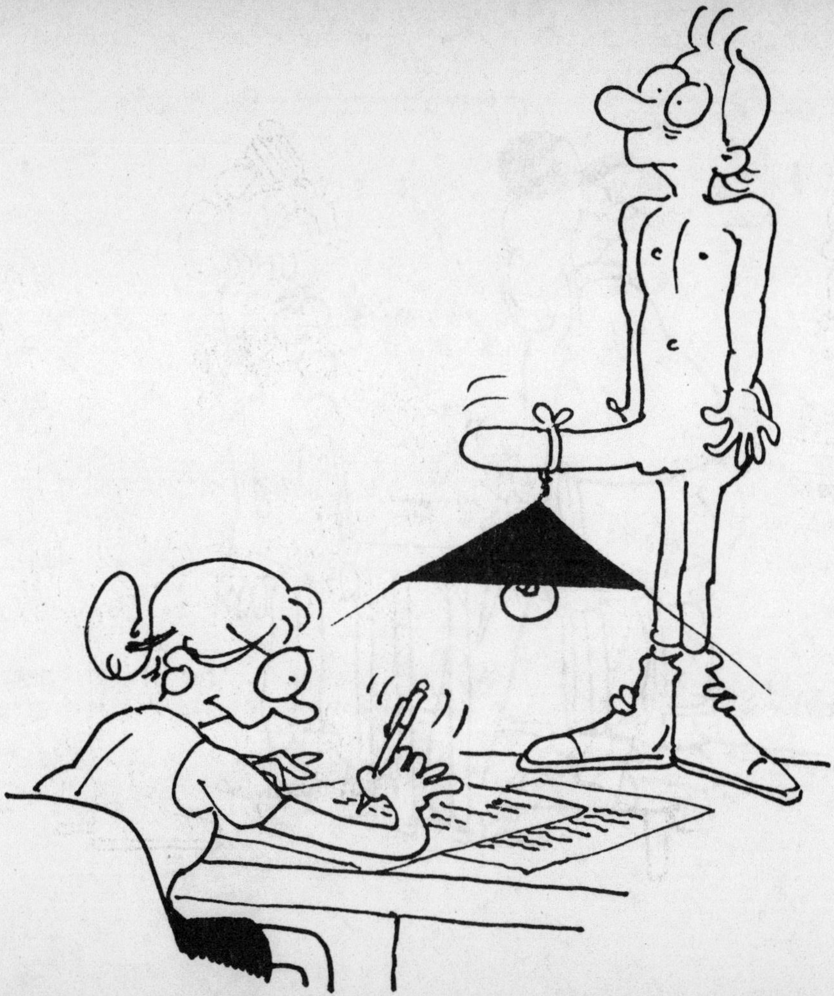

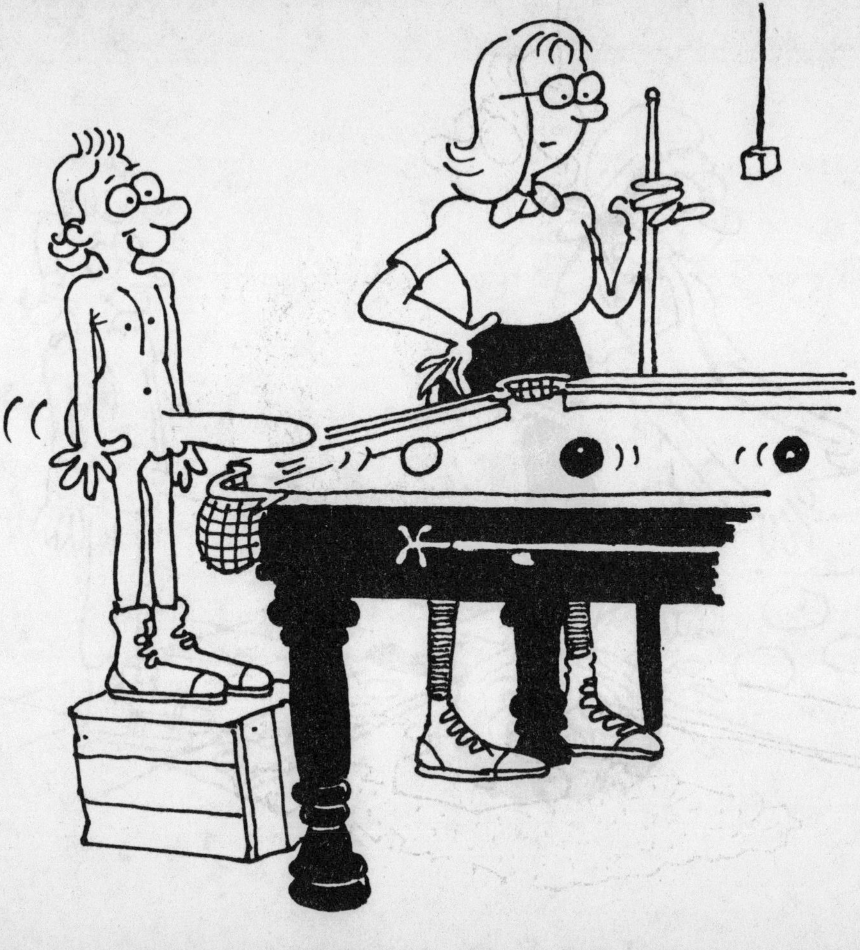

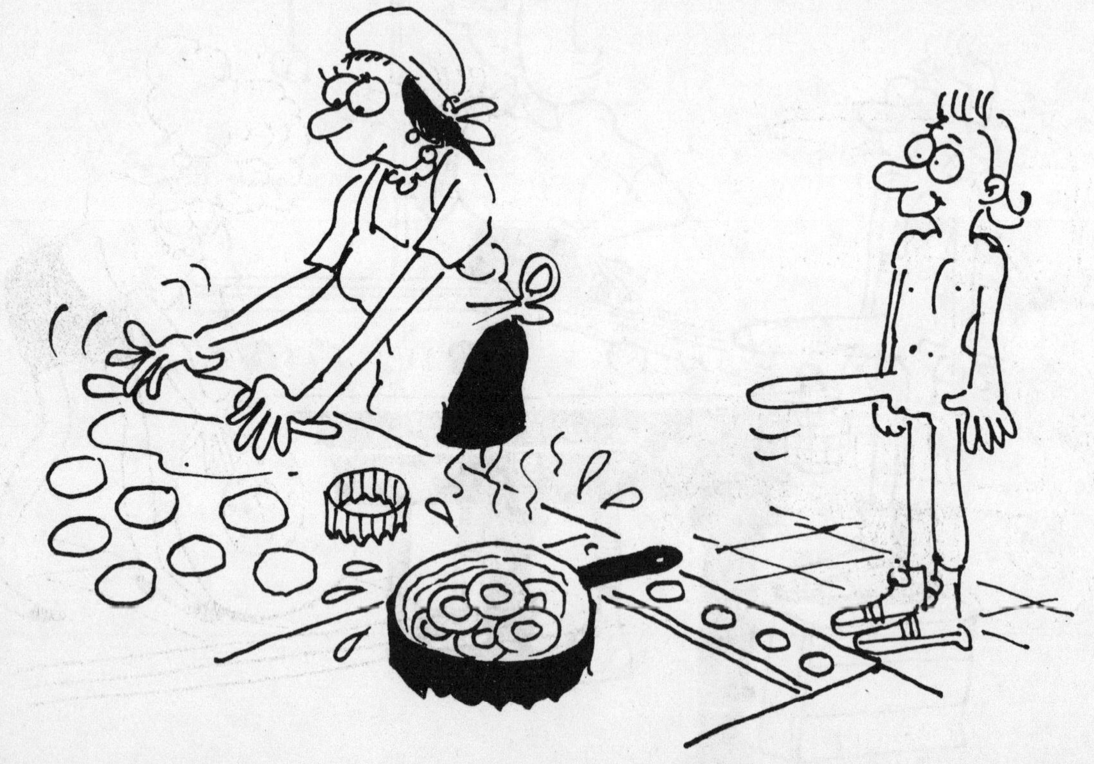

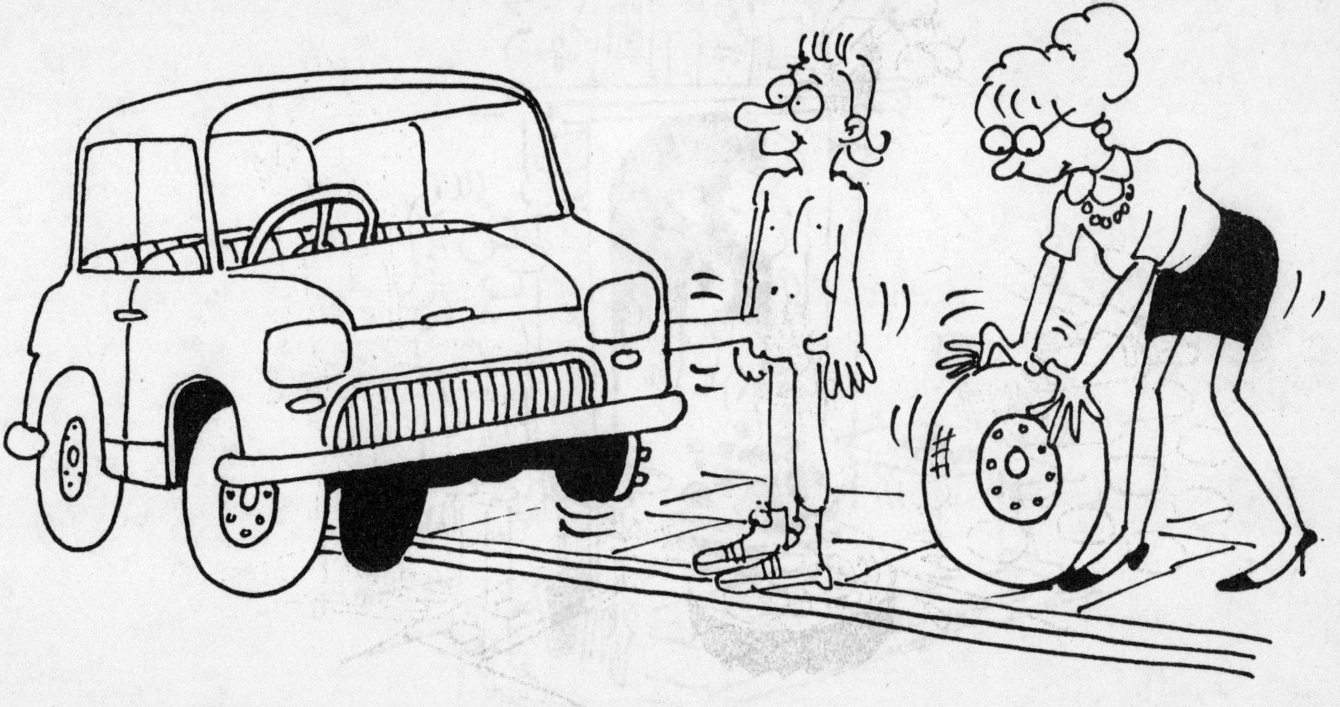

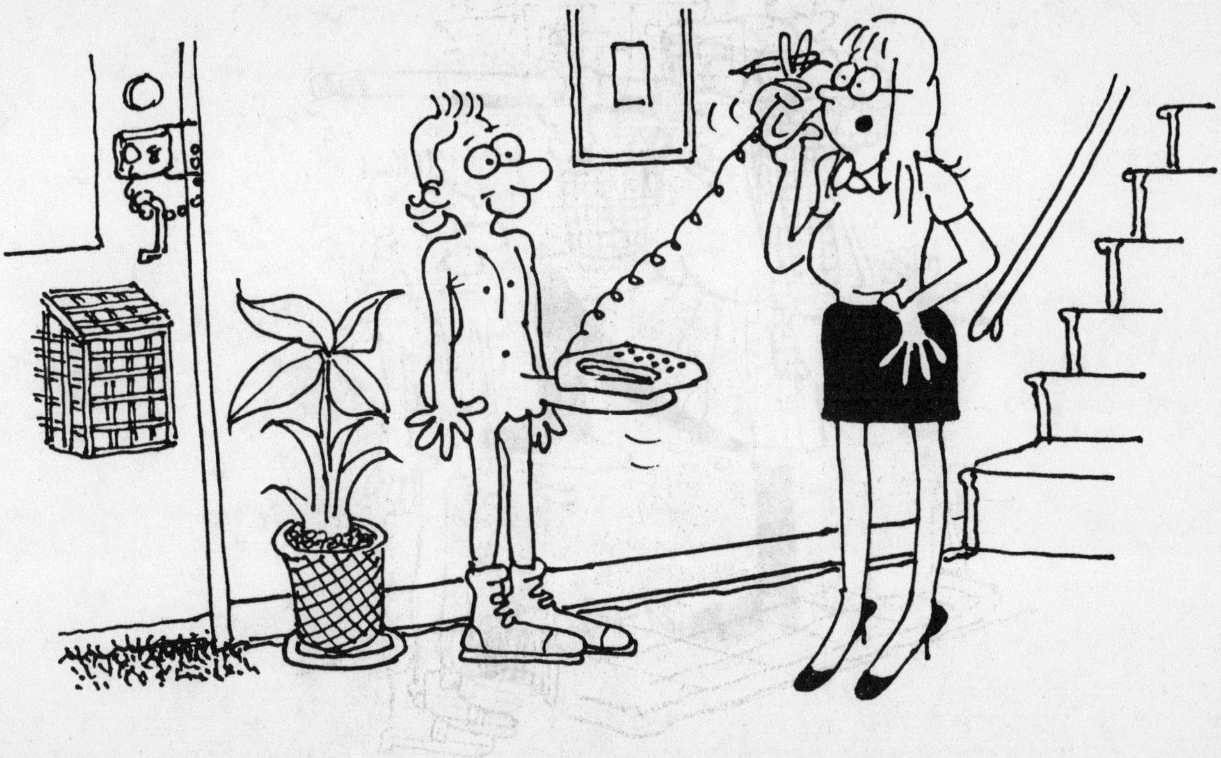

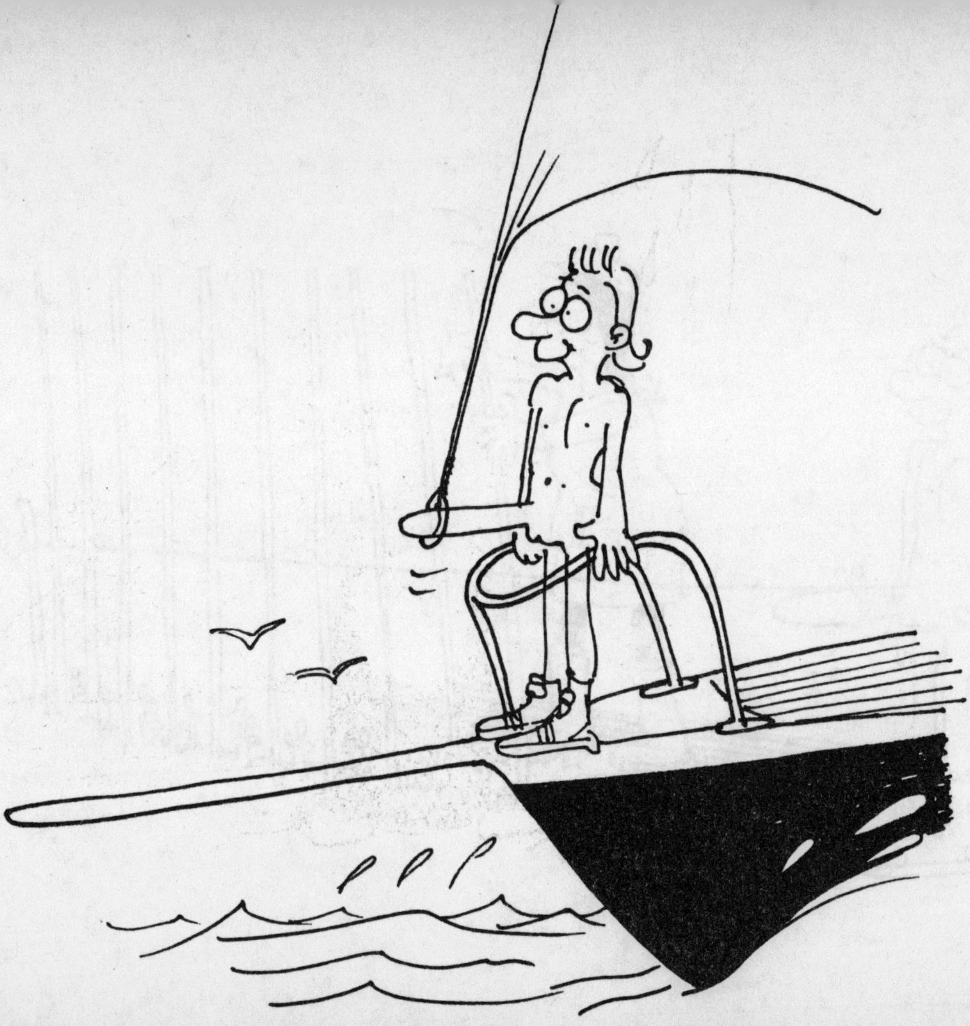

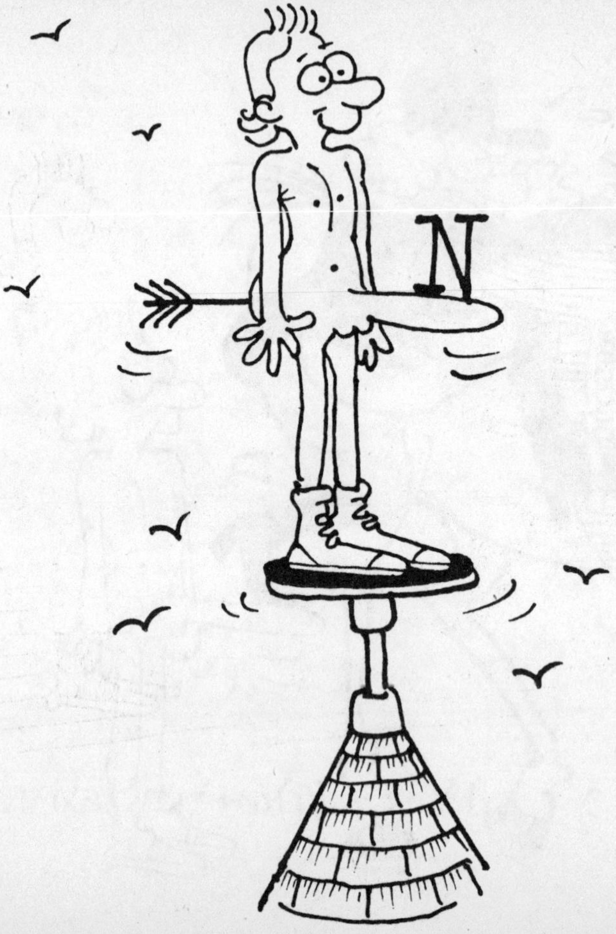
N

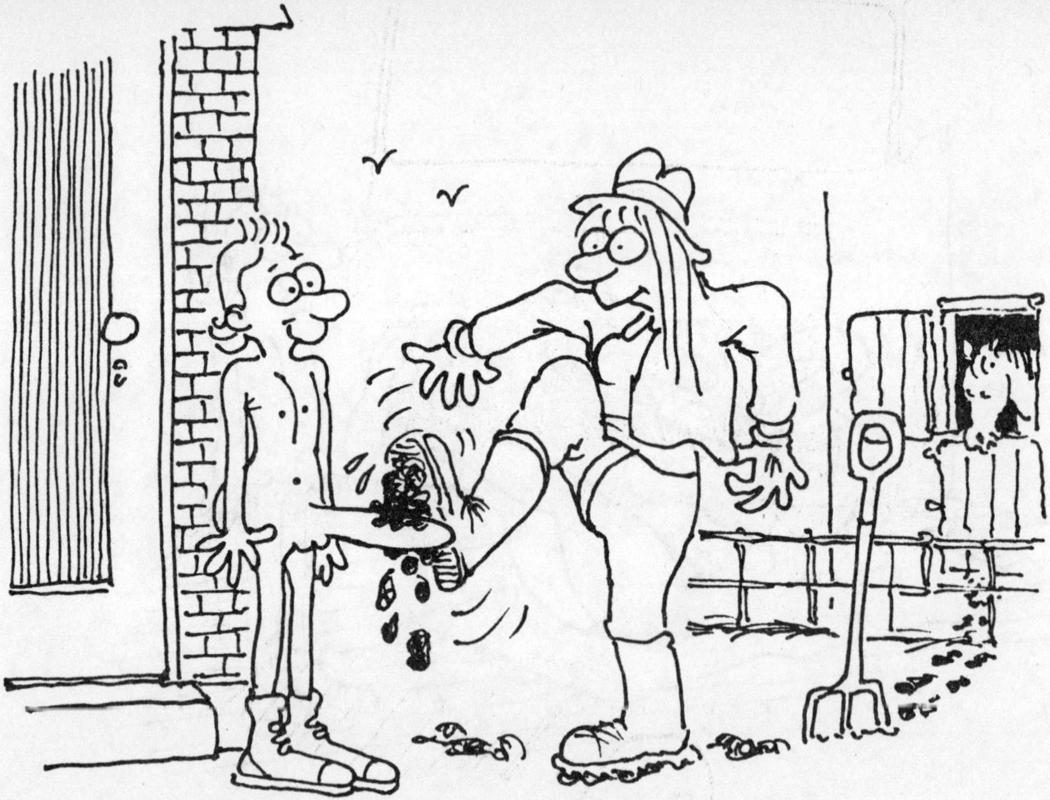

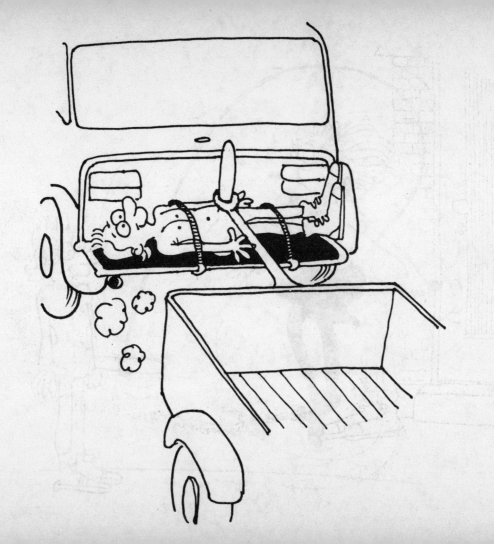

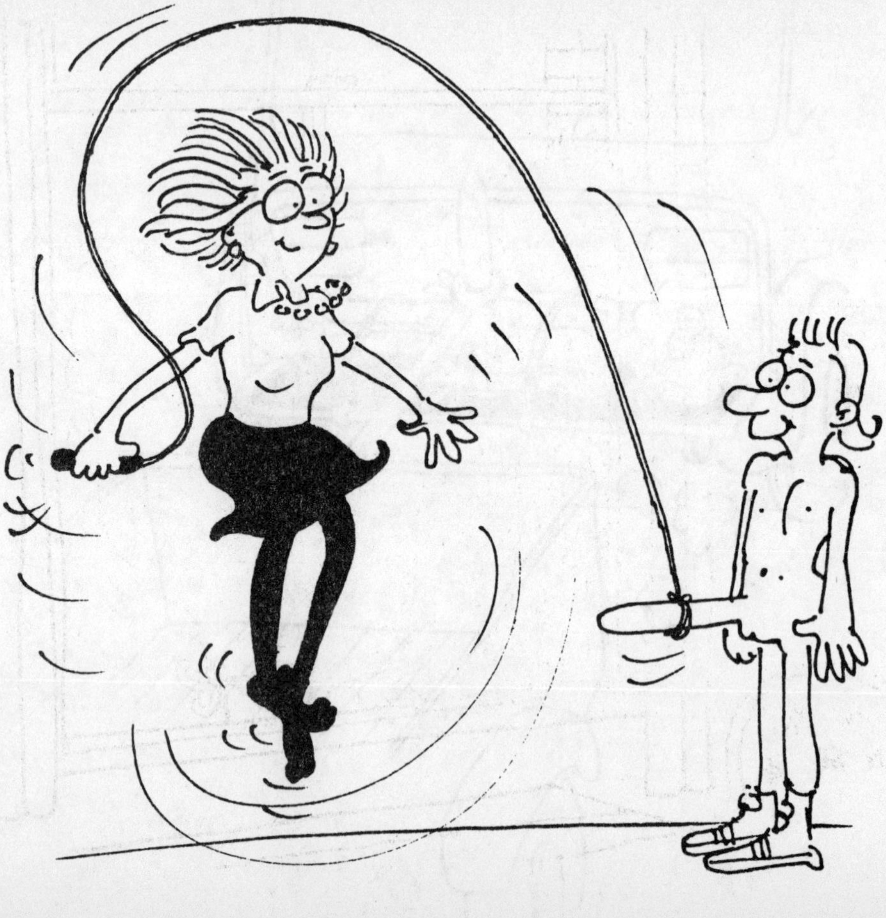

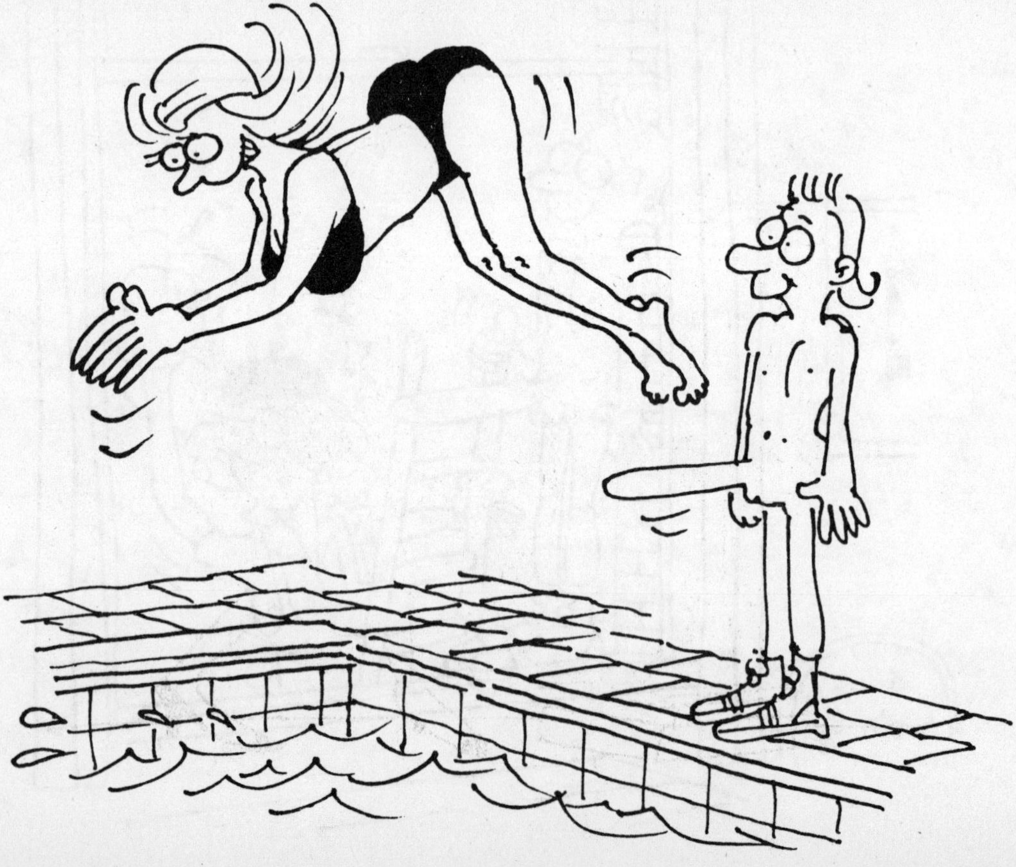

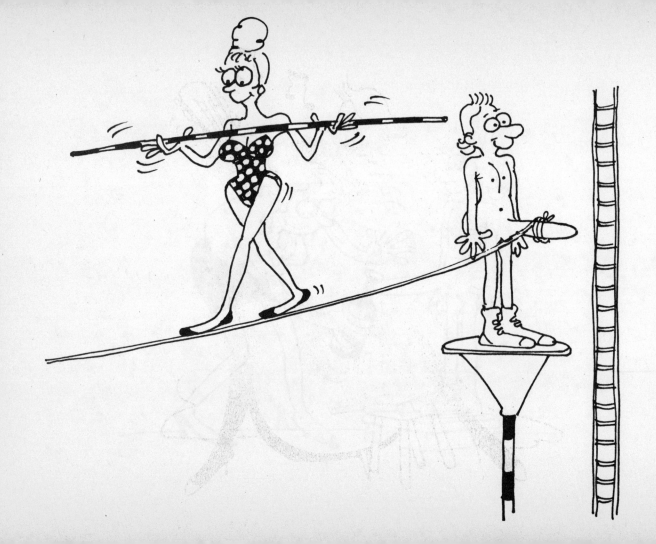

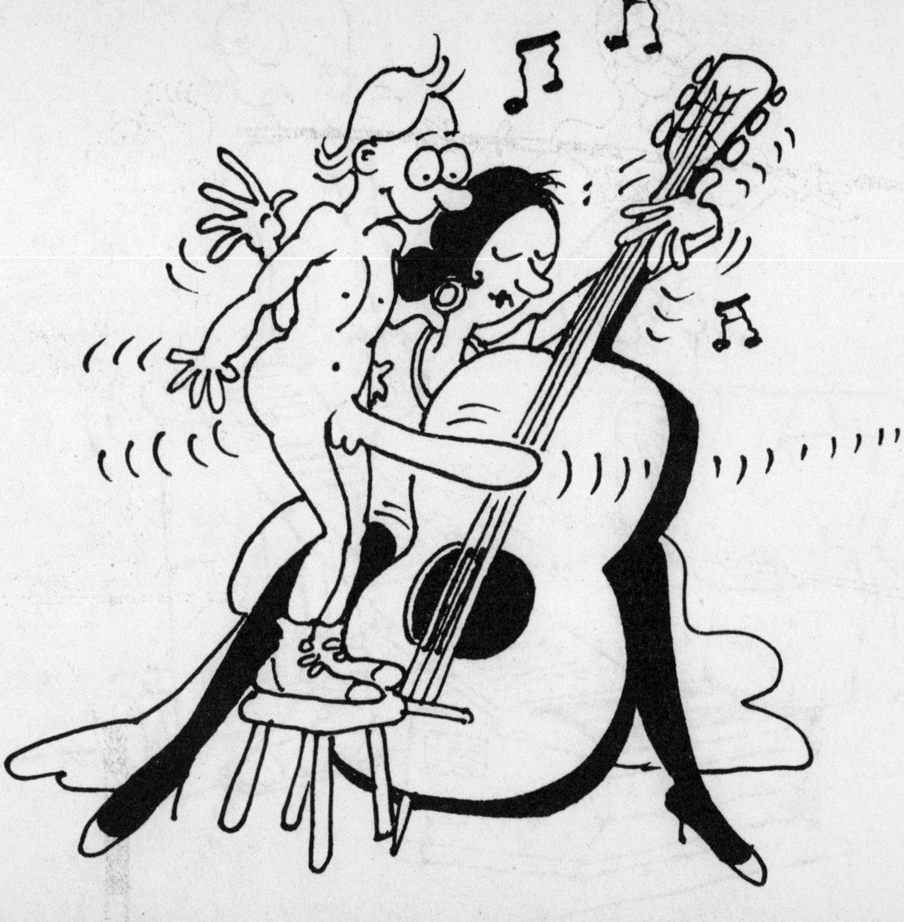

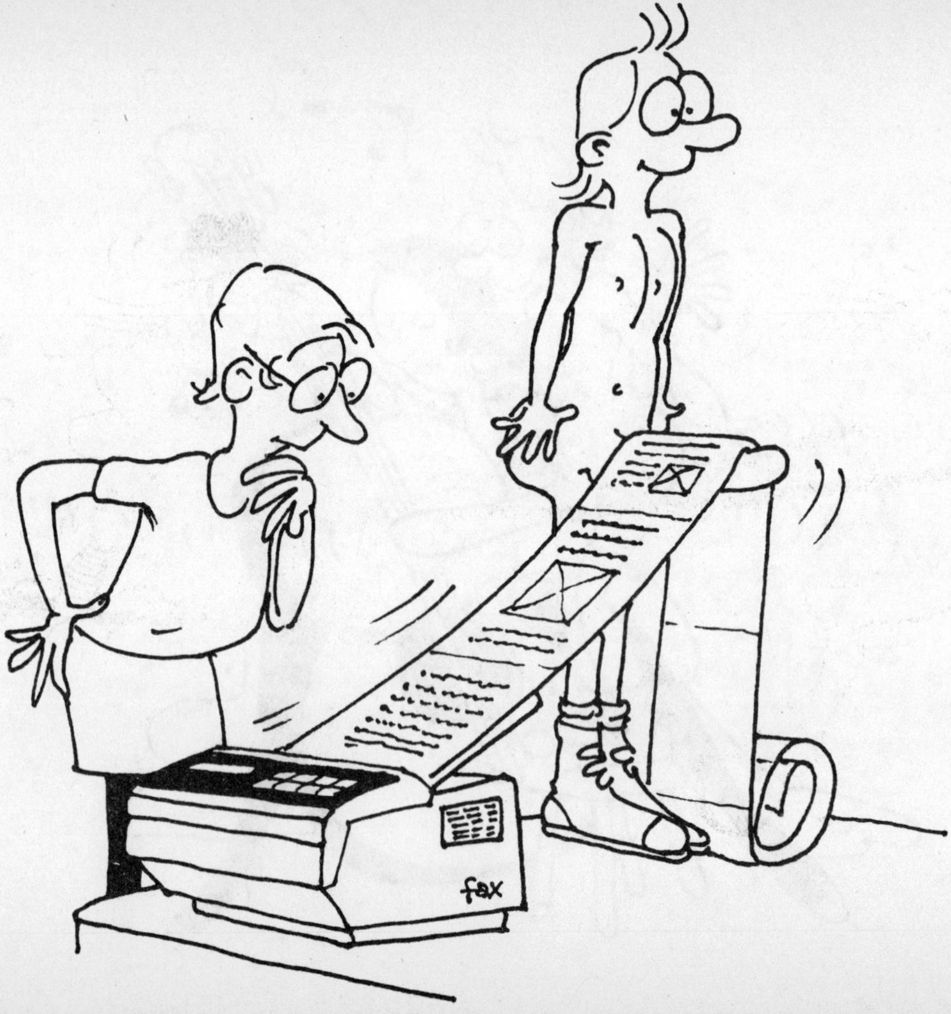
fax

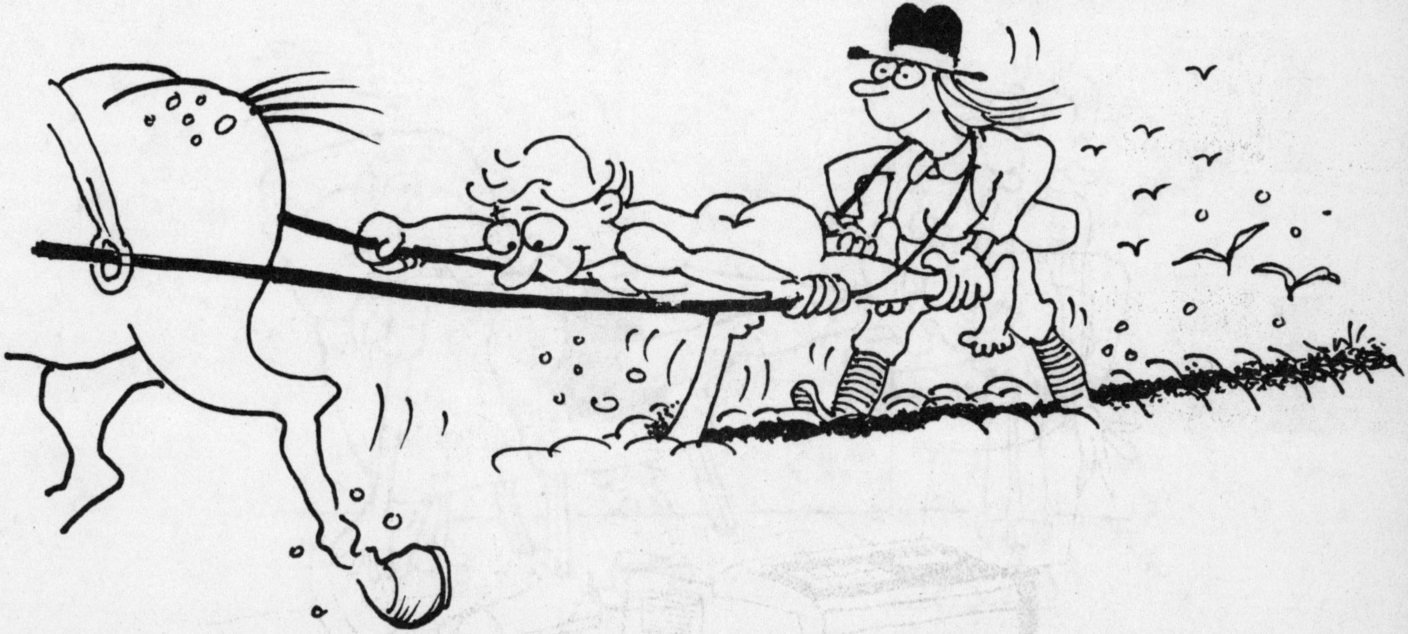

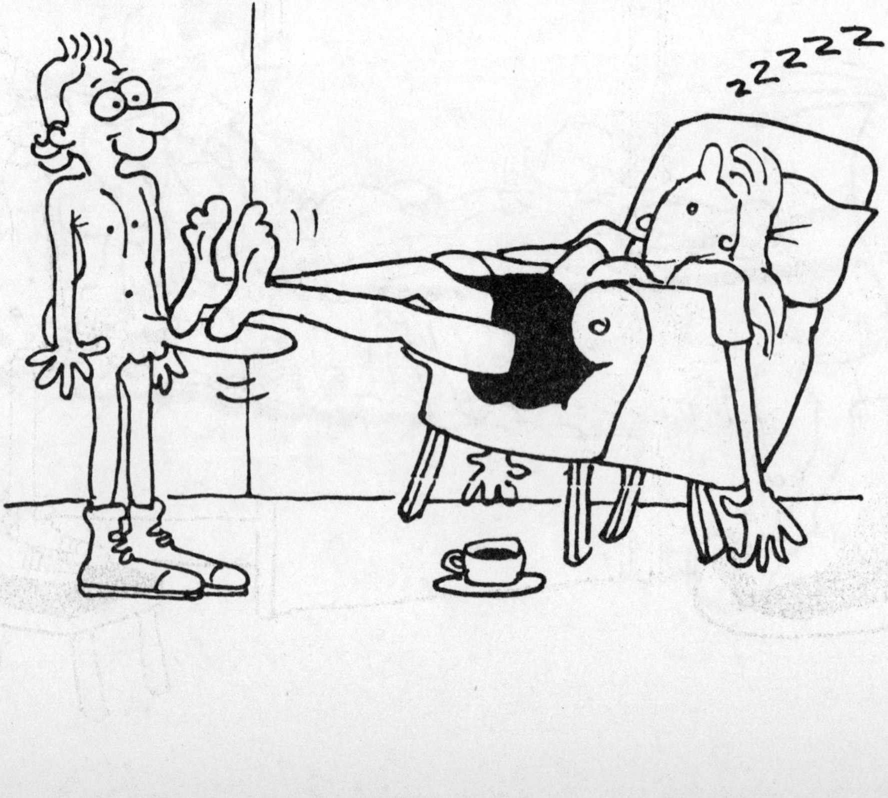
ZZZZZZ

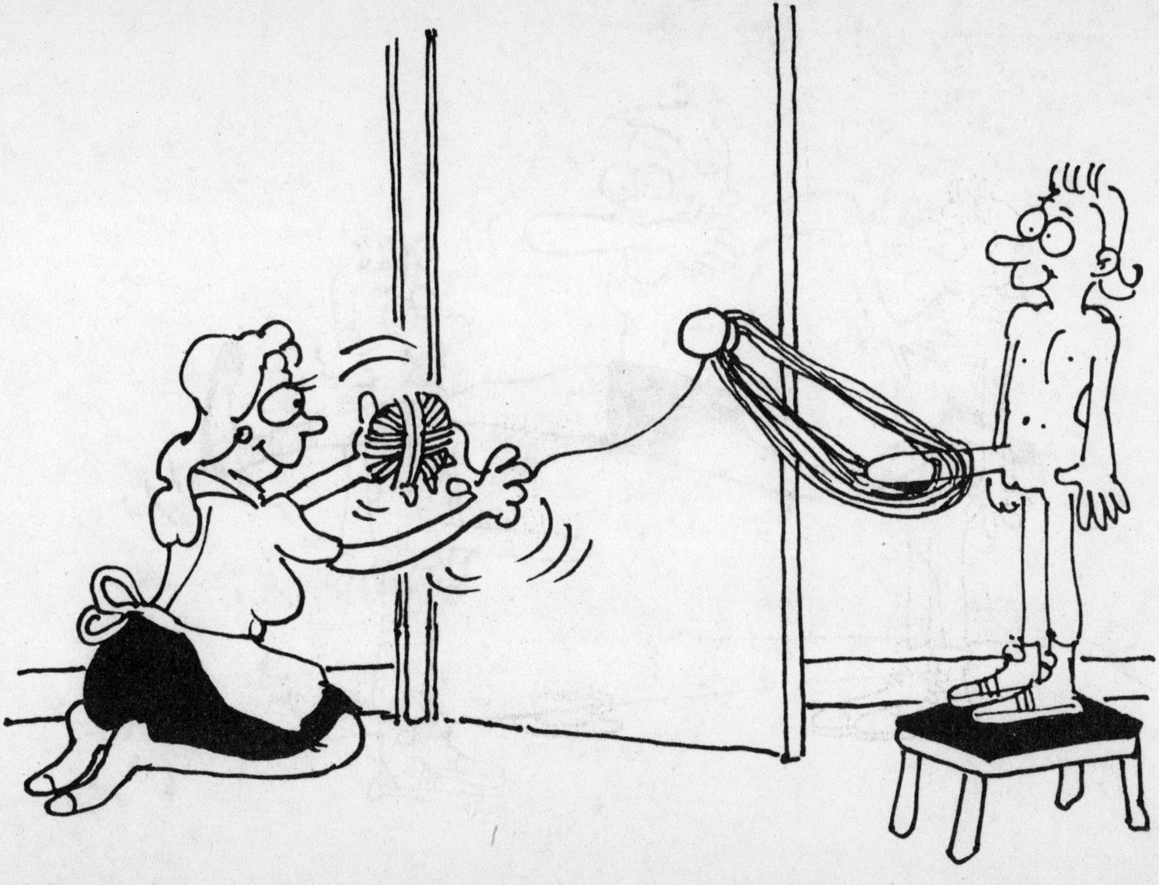

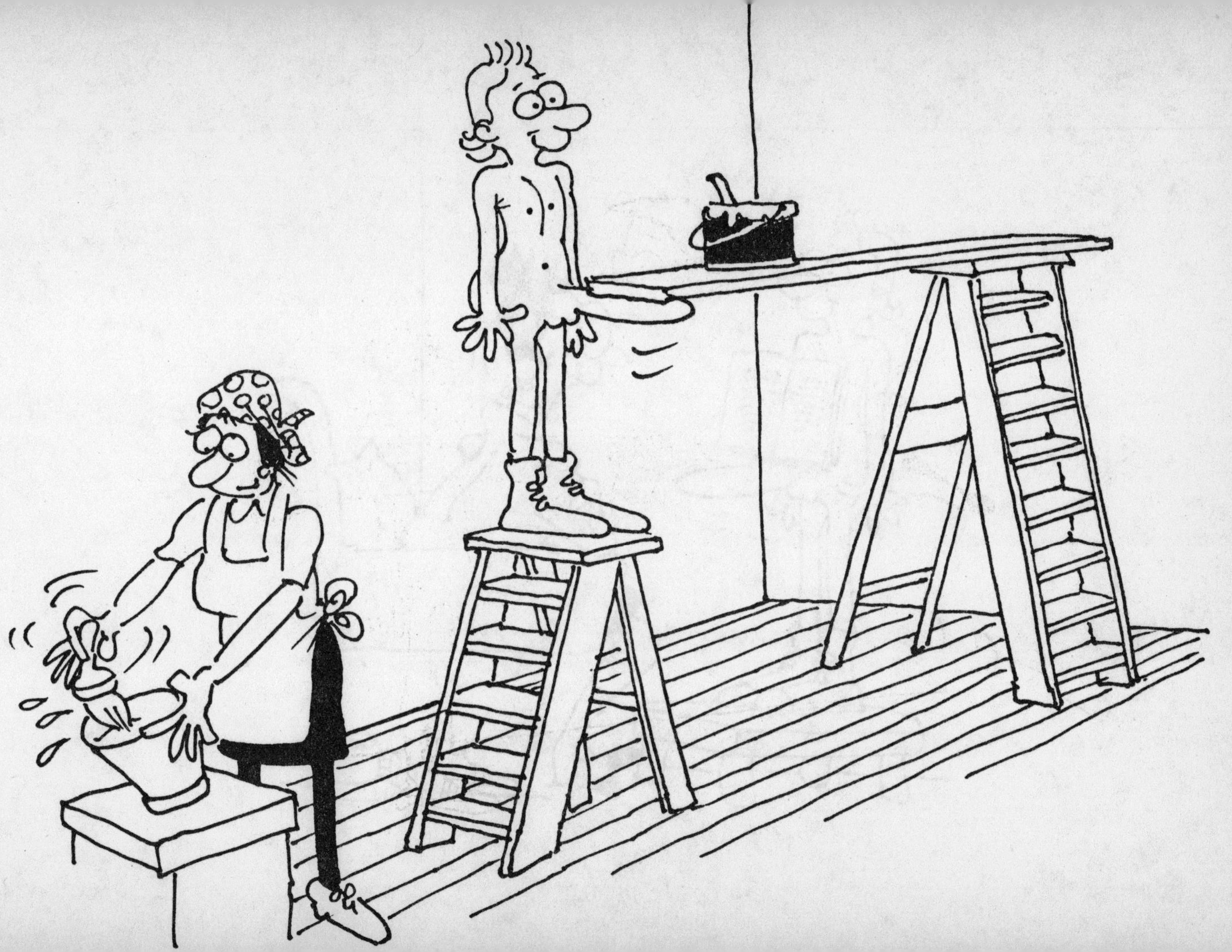

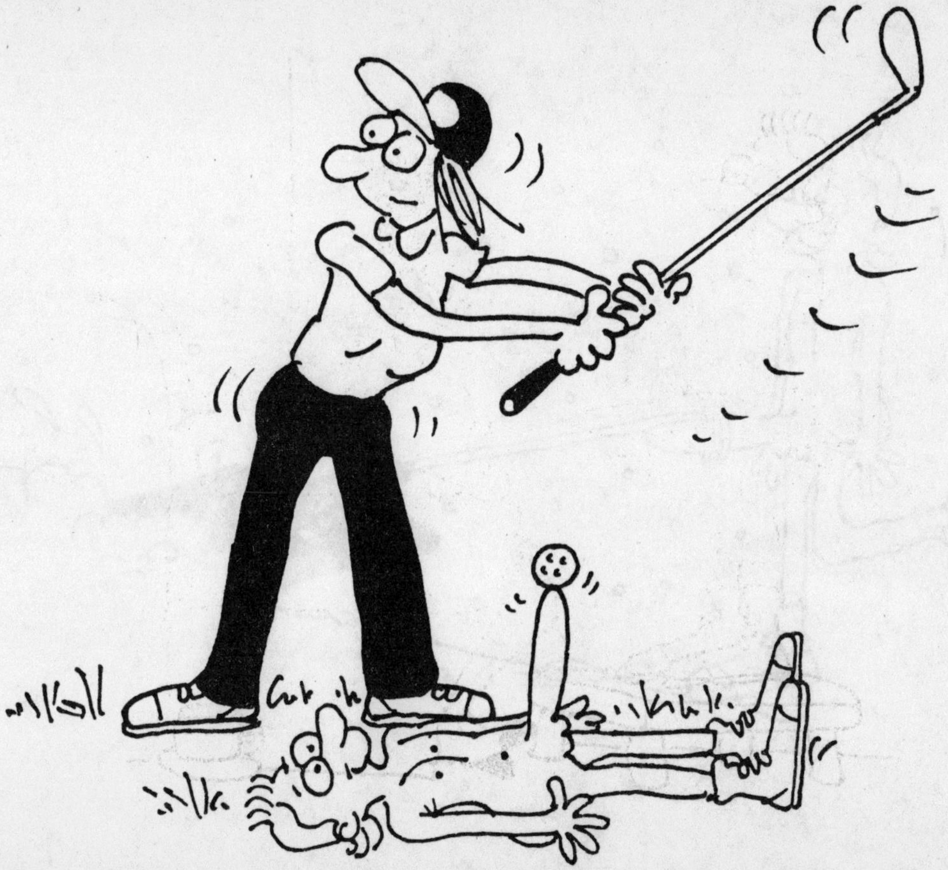

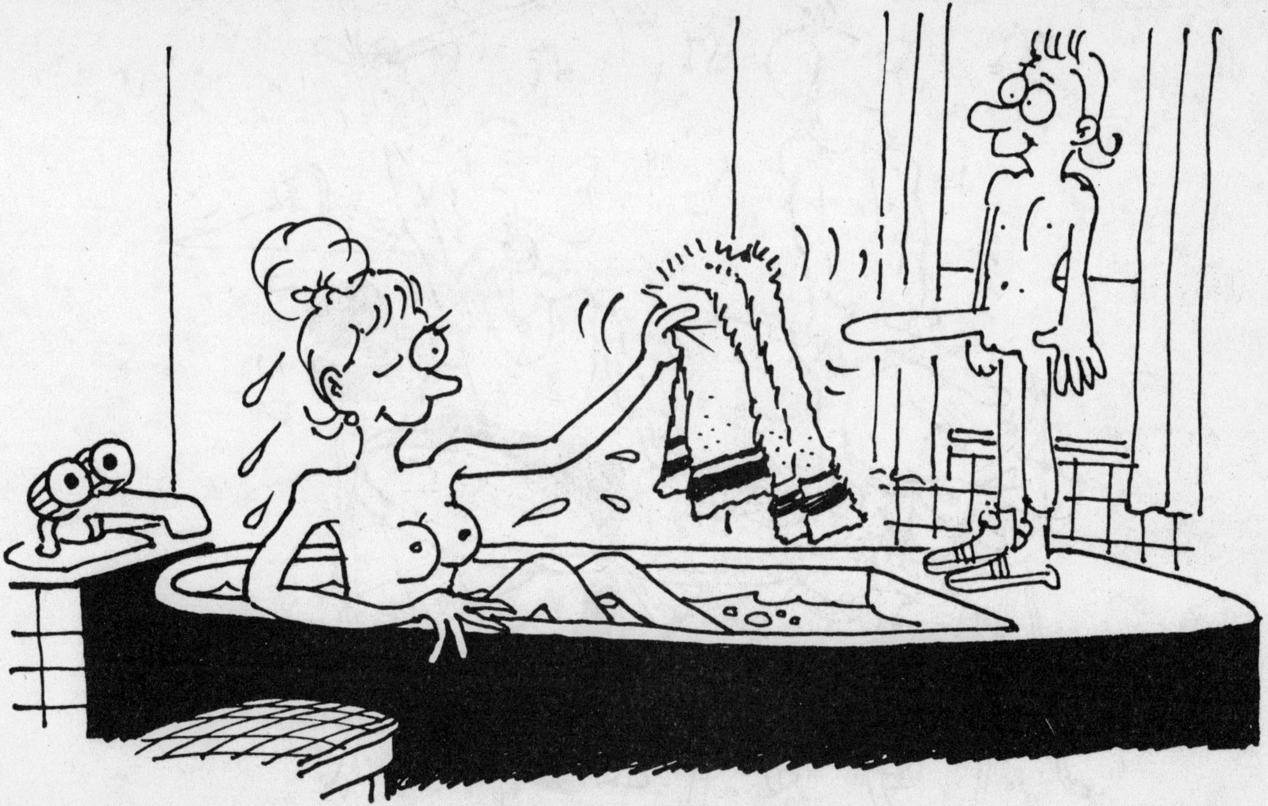

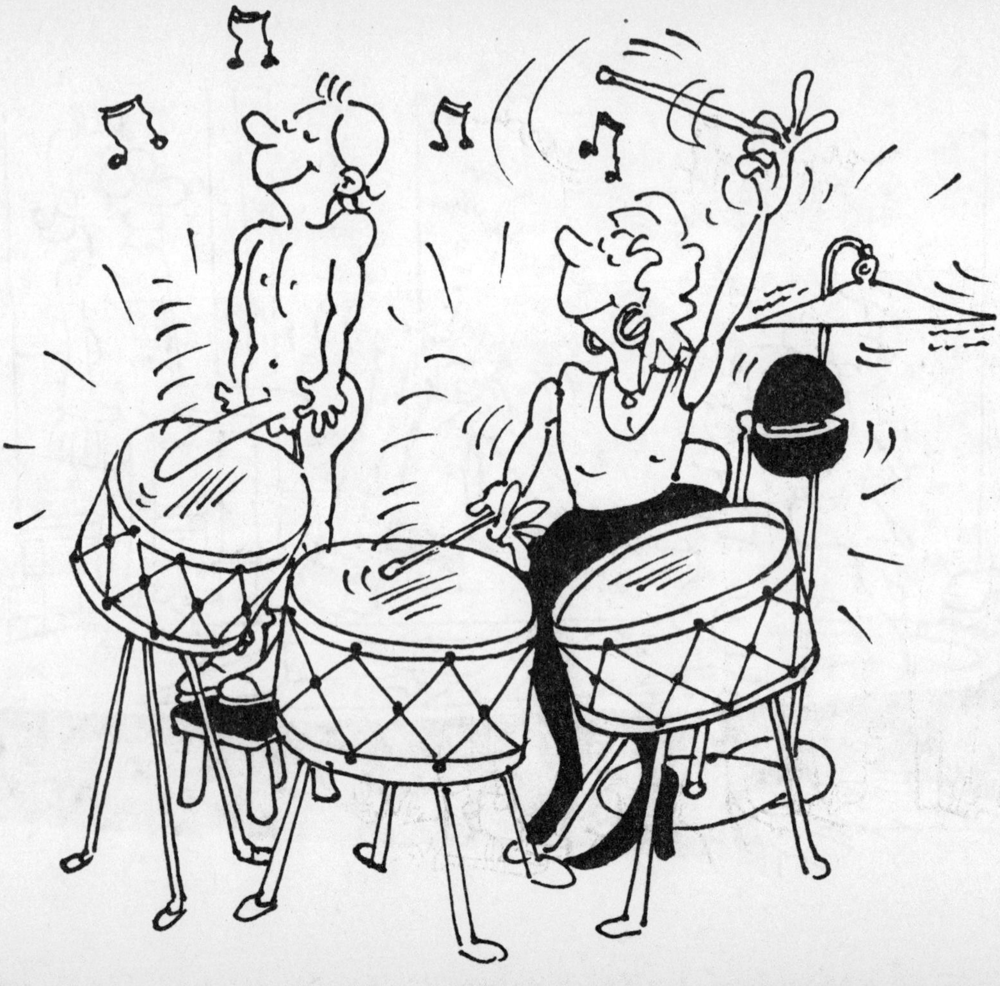

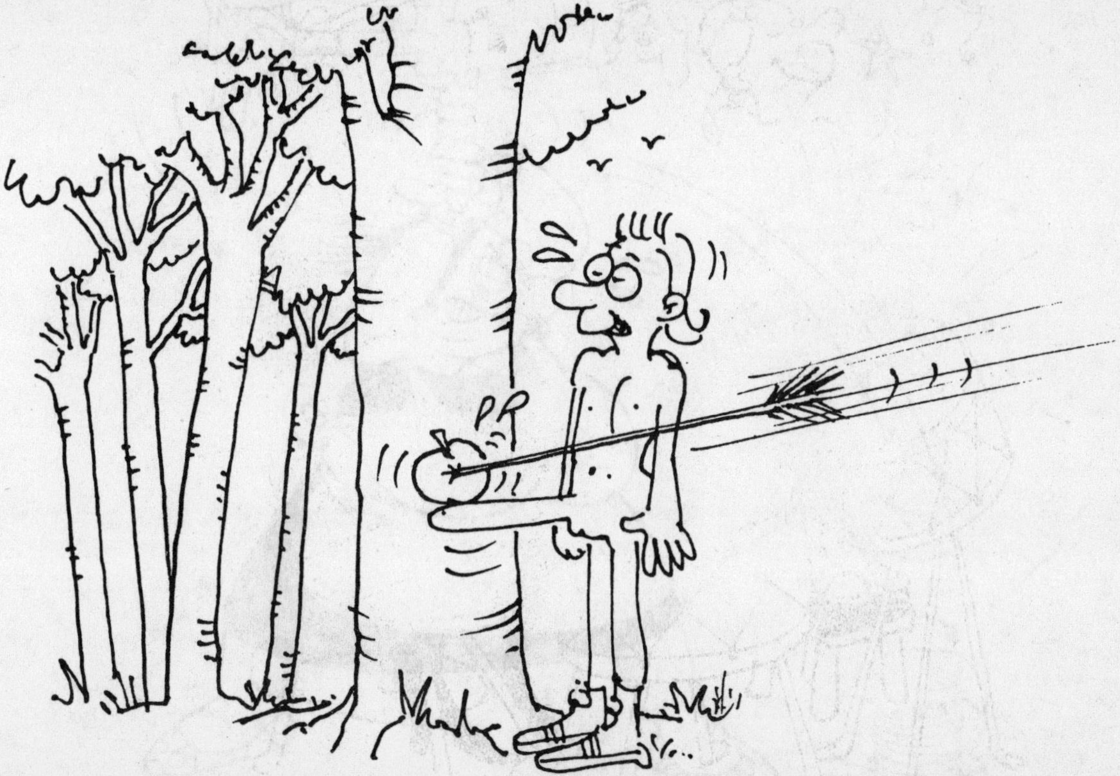

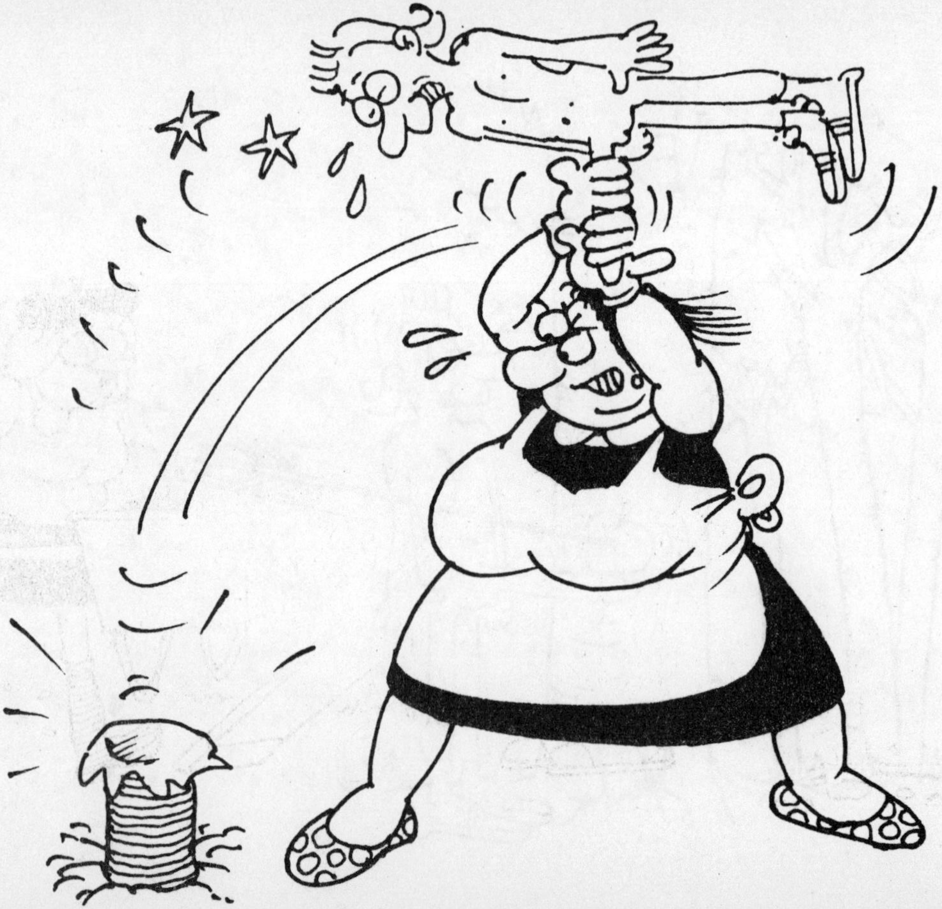

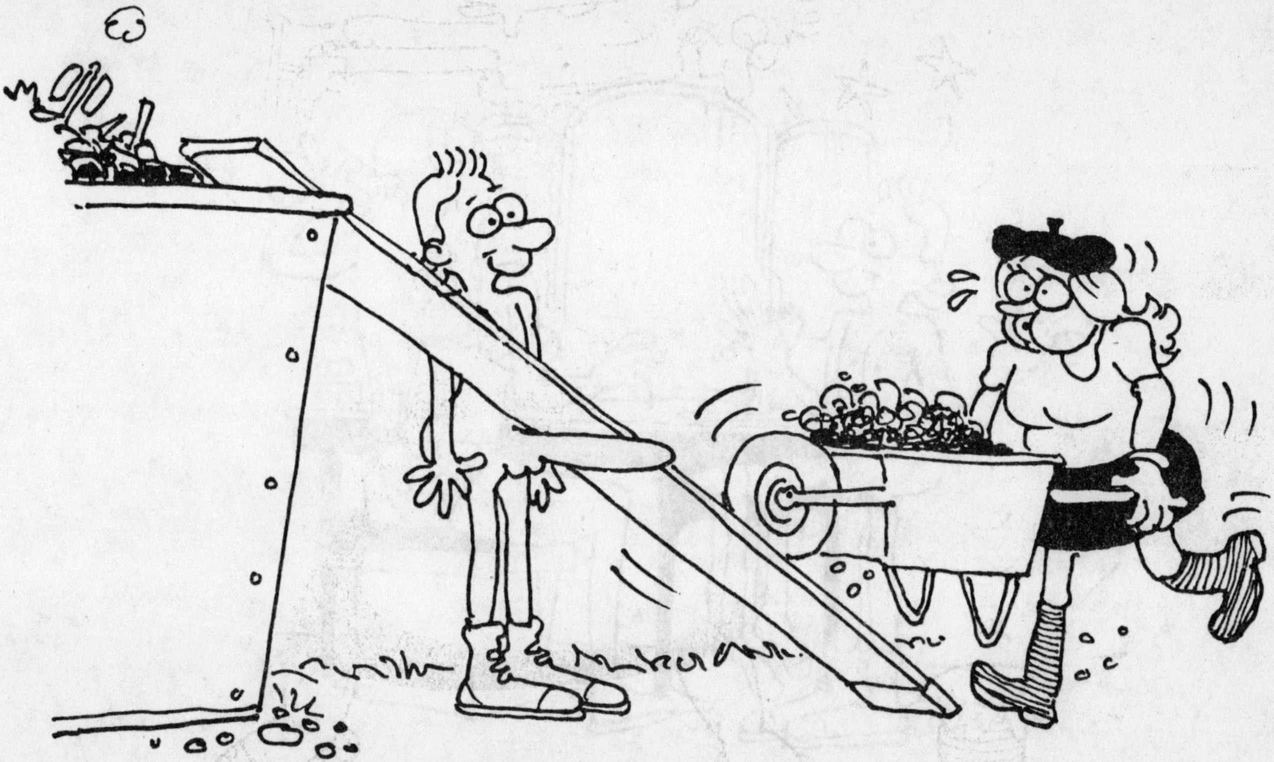

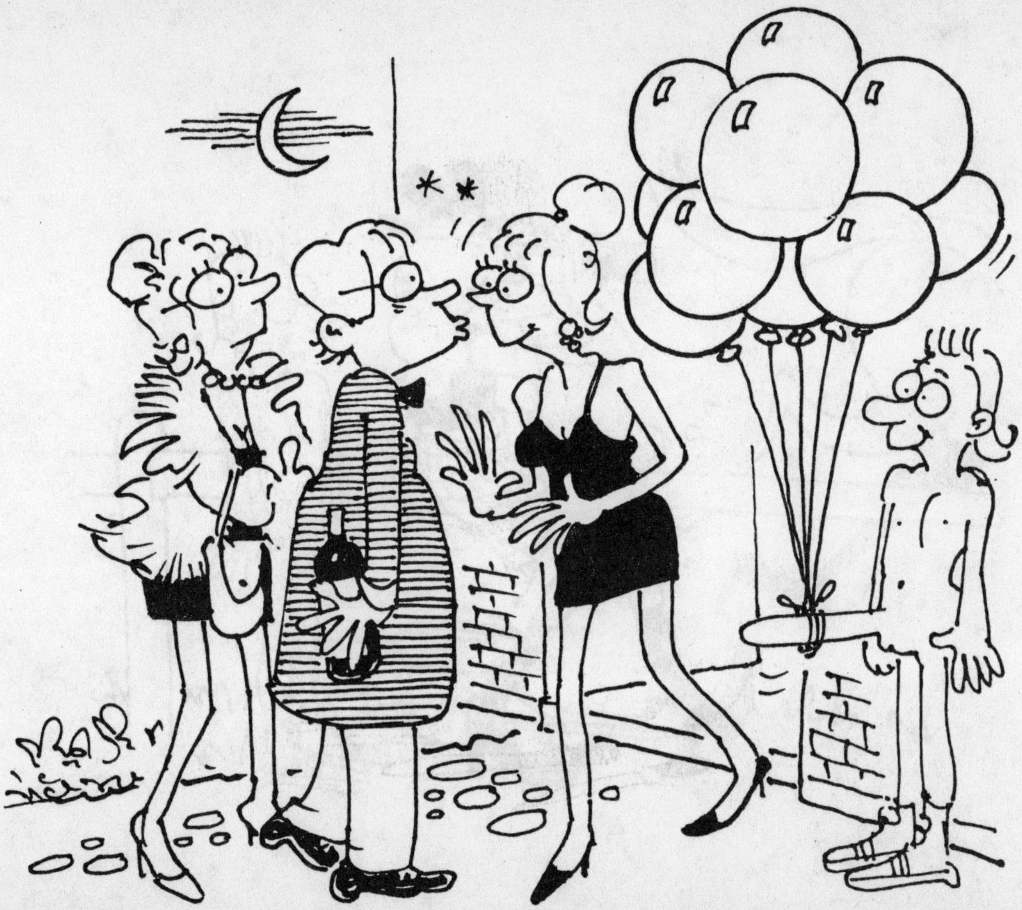

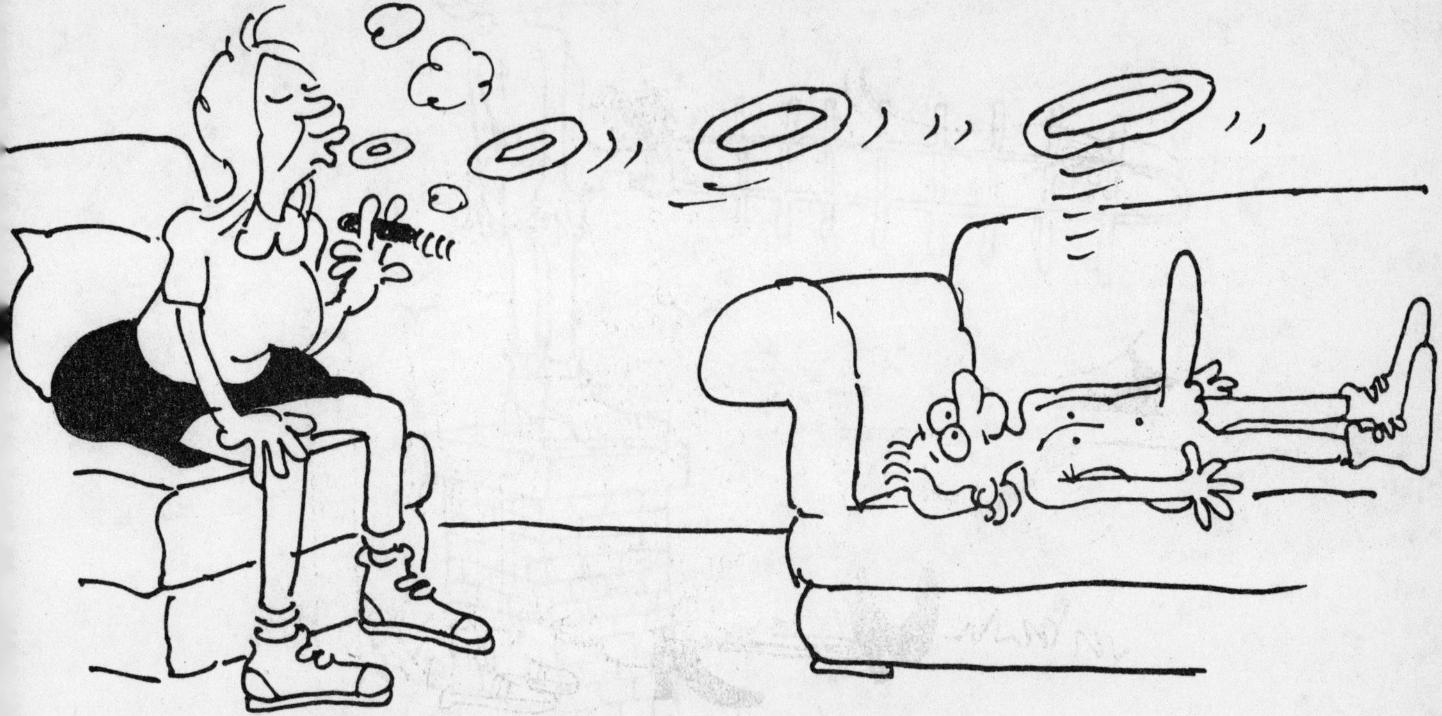

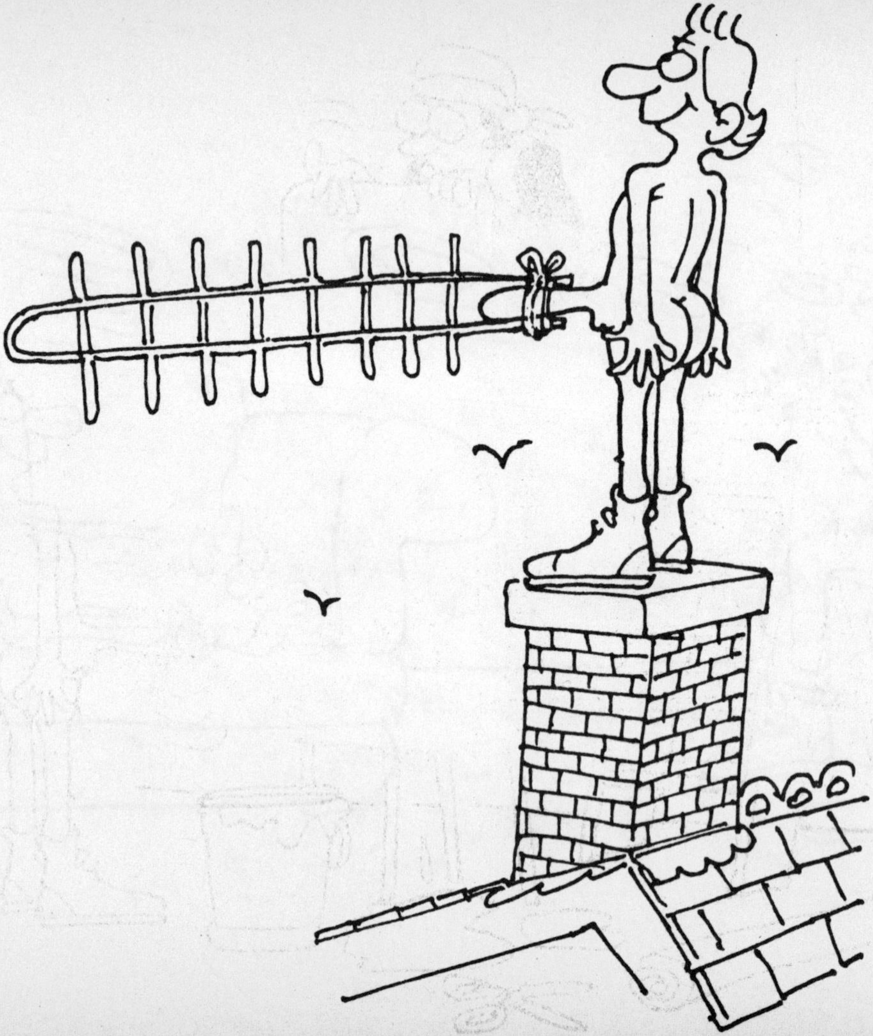

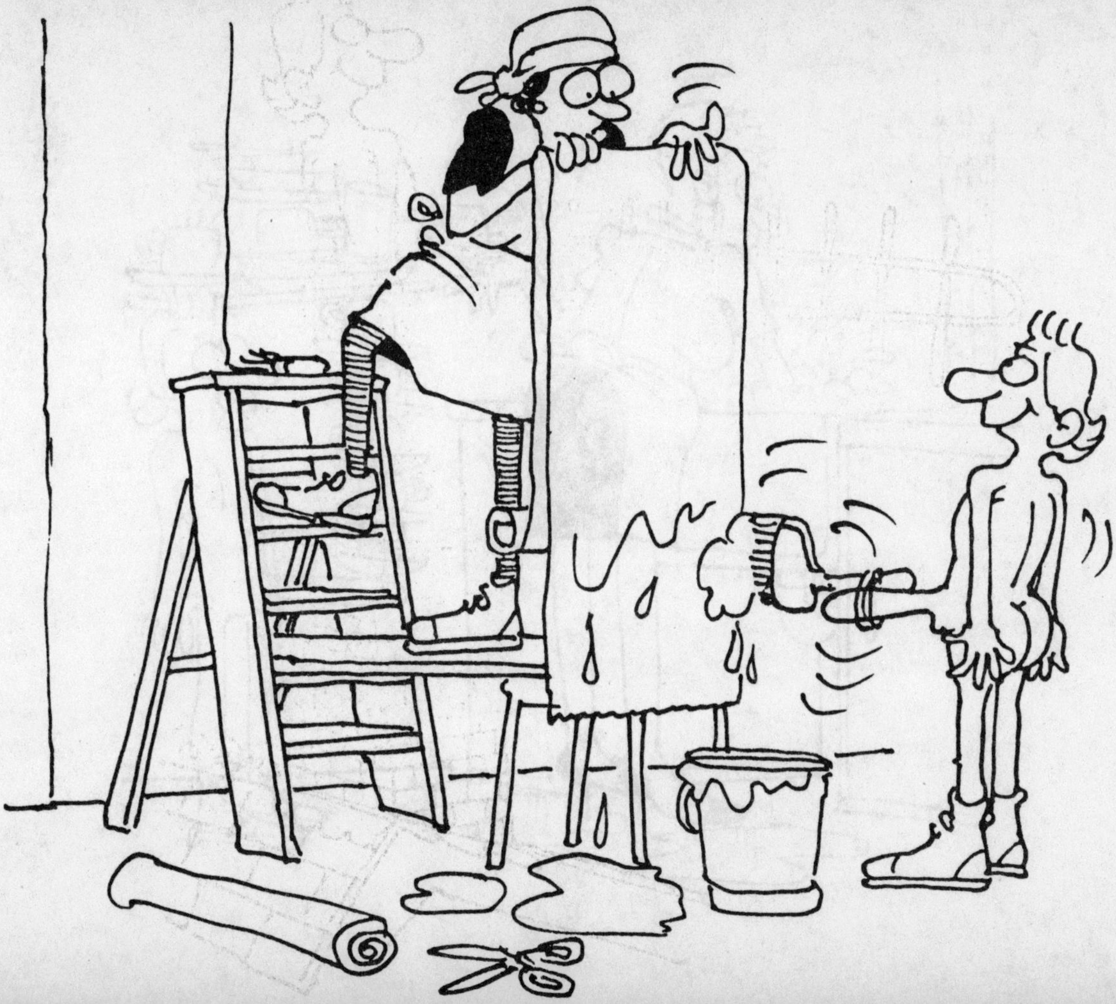

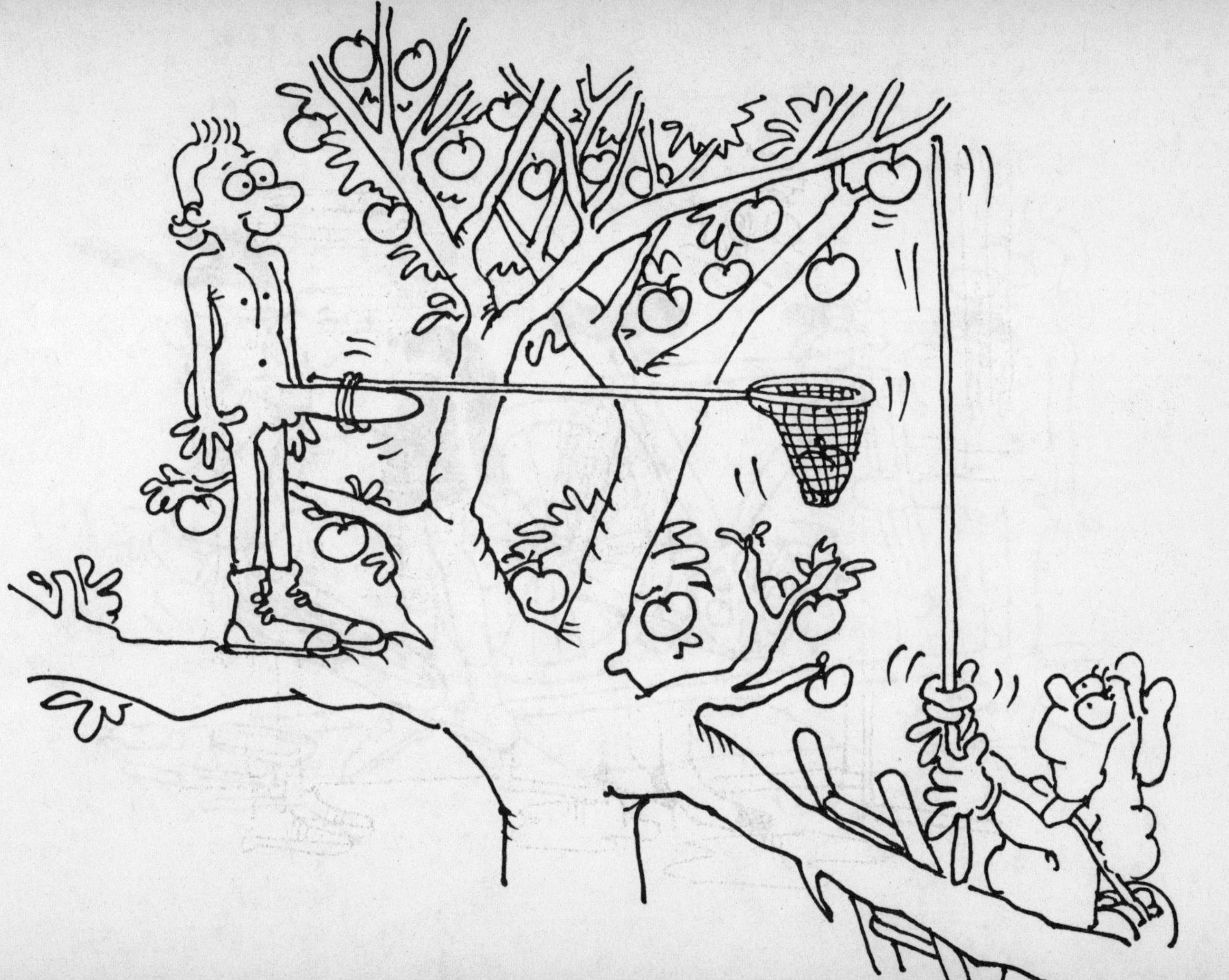

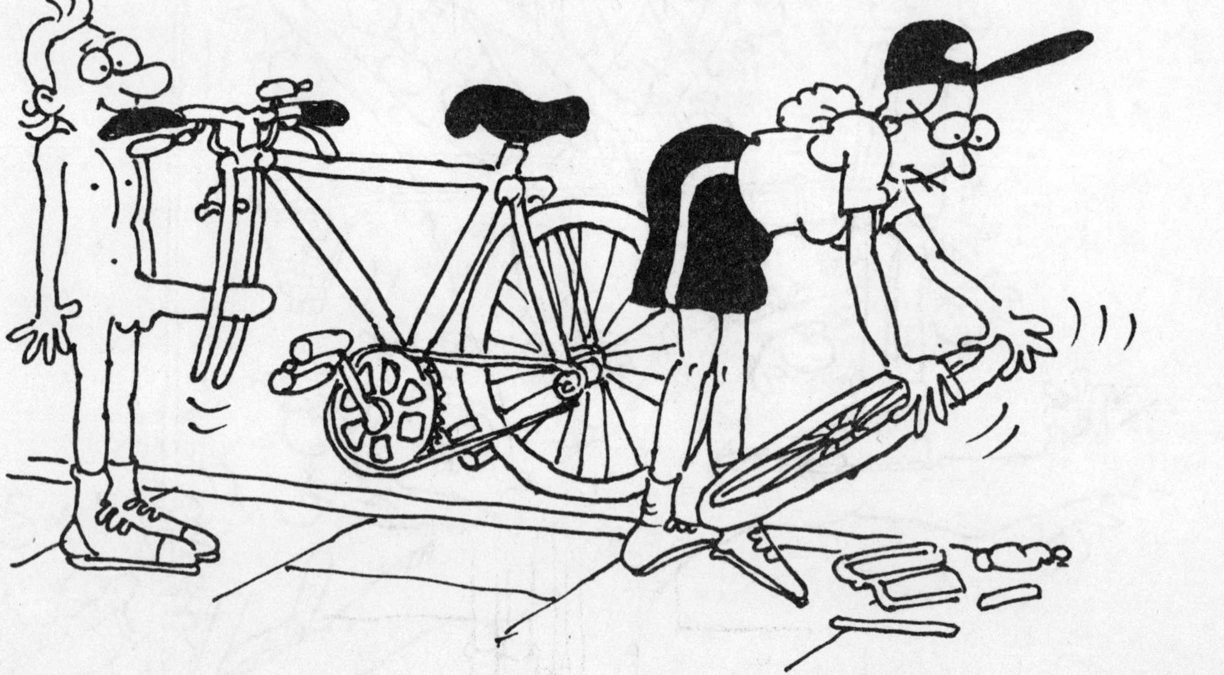

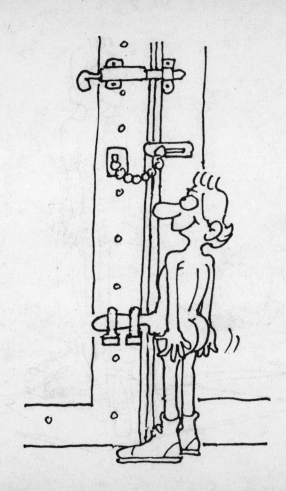

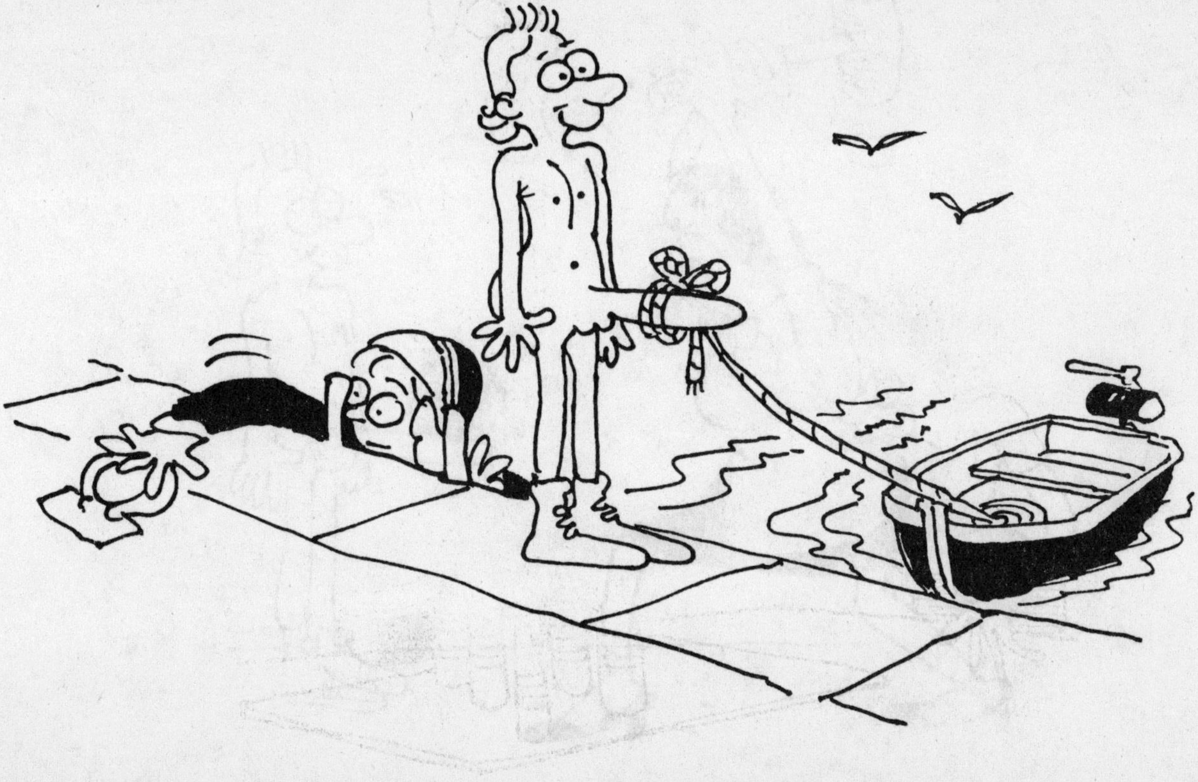

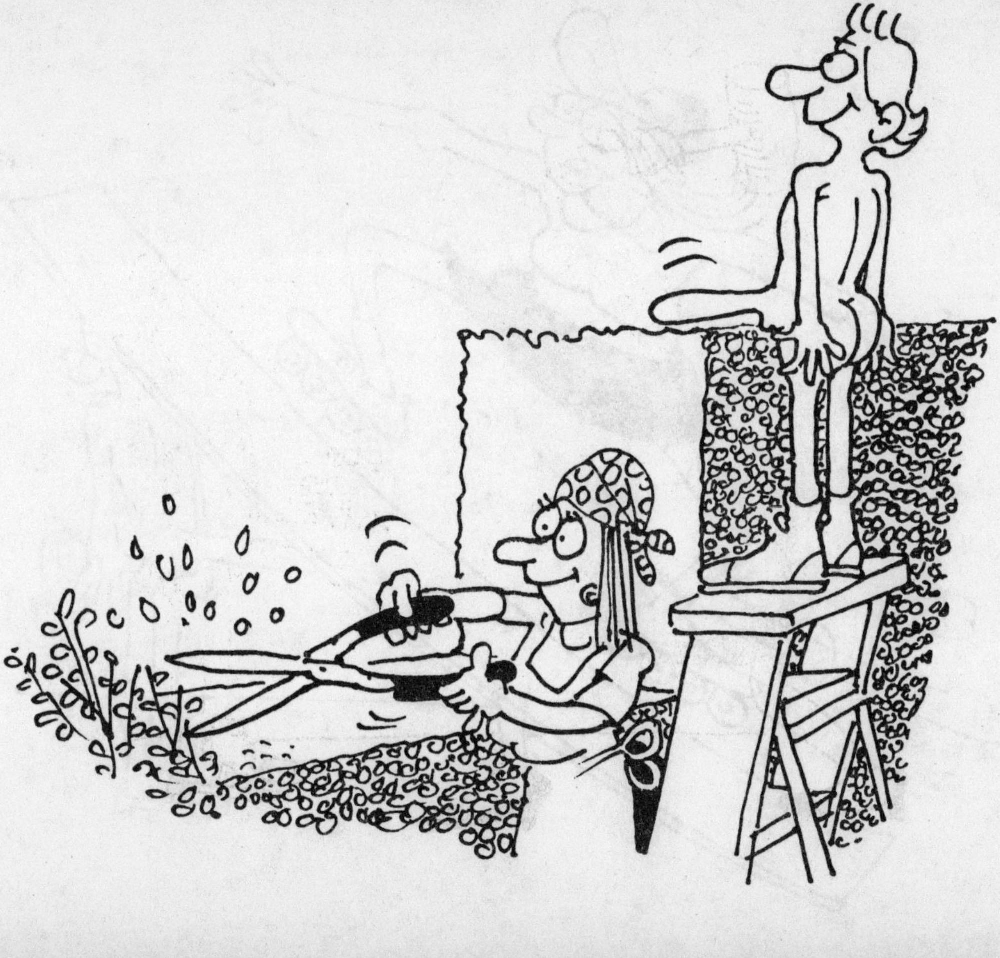

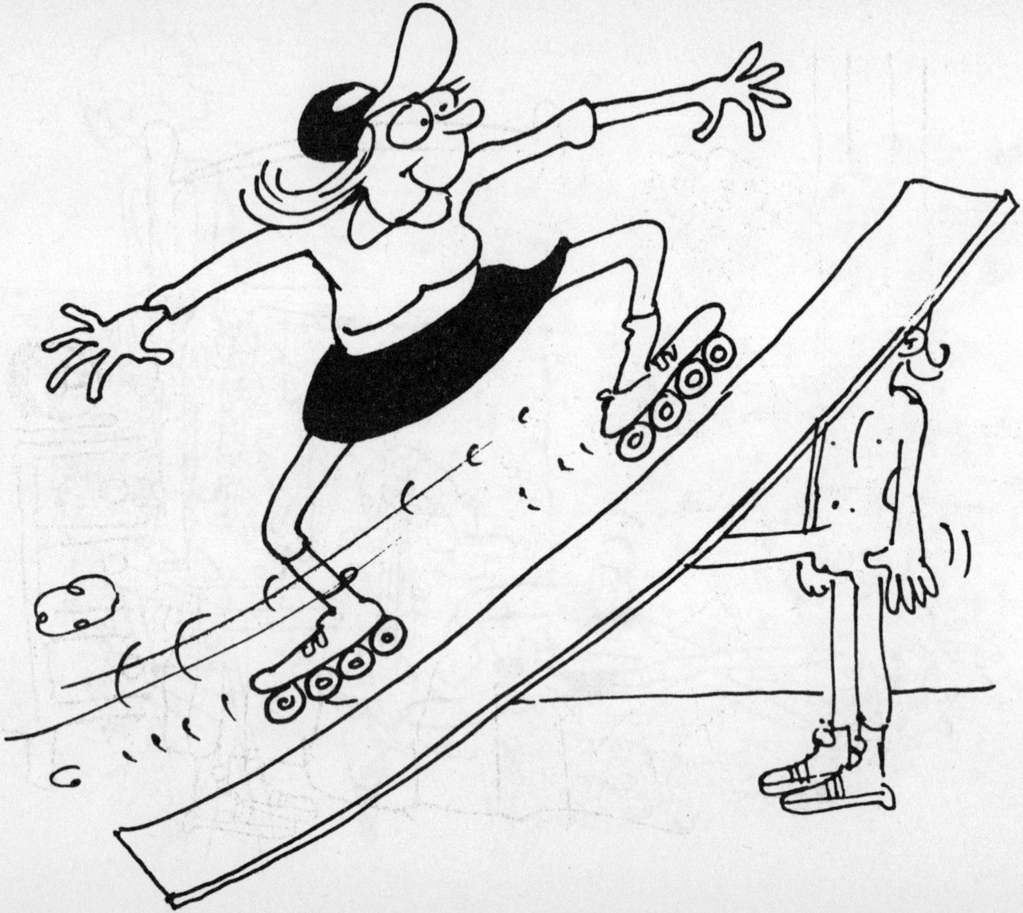

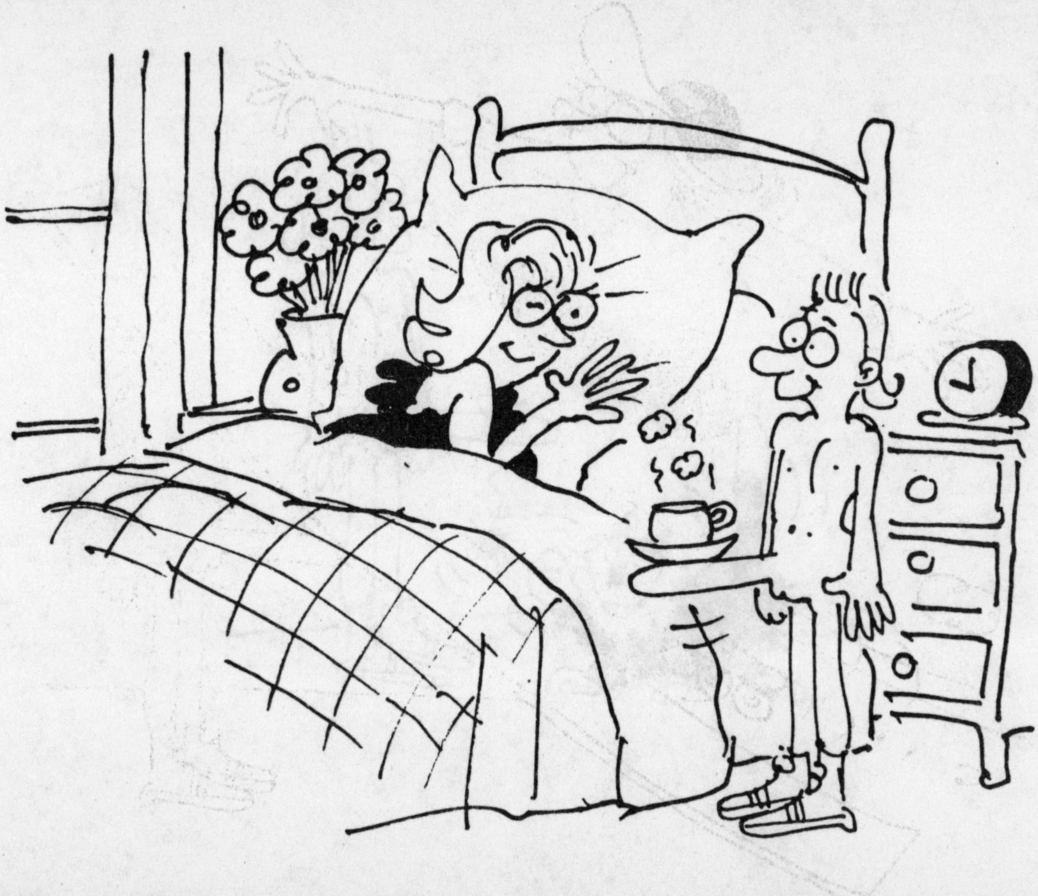

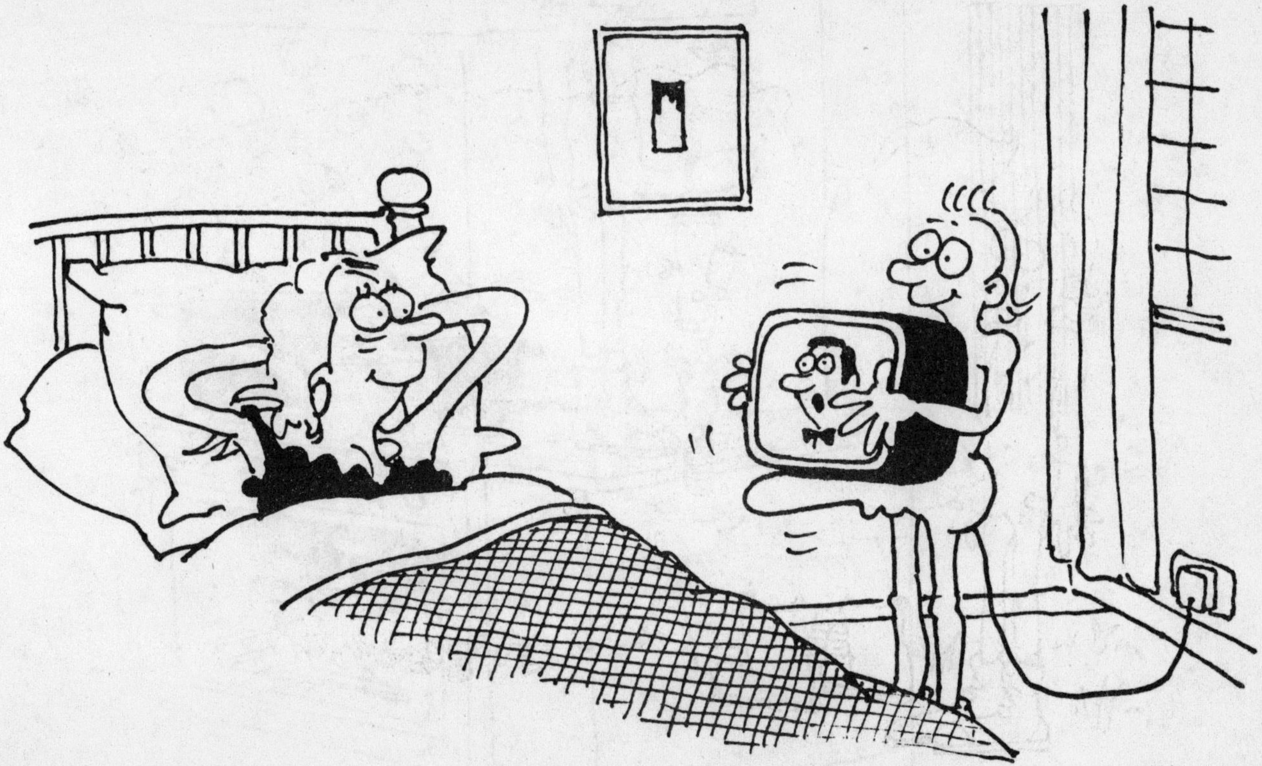

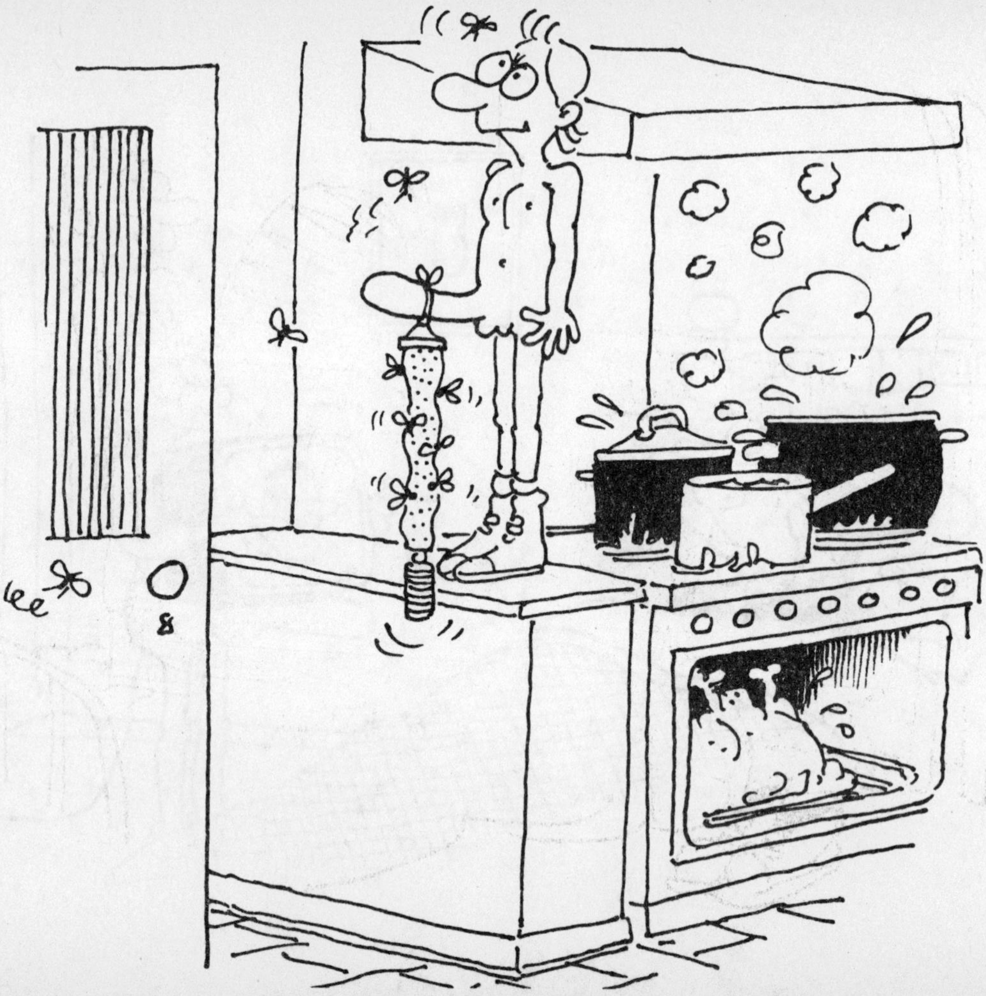

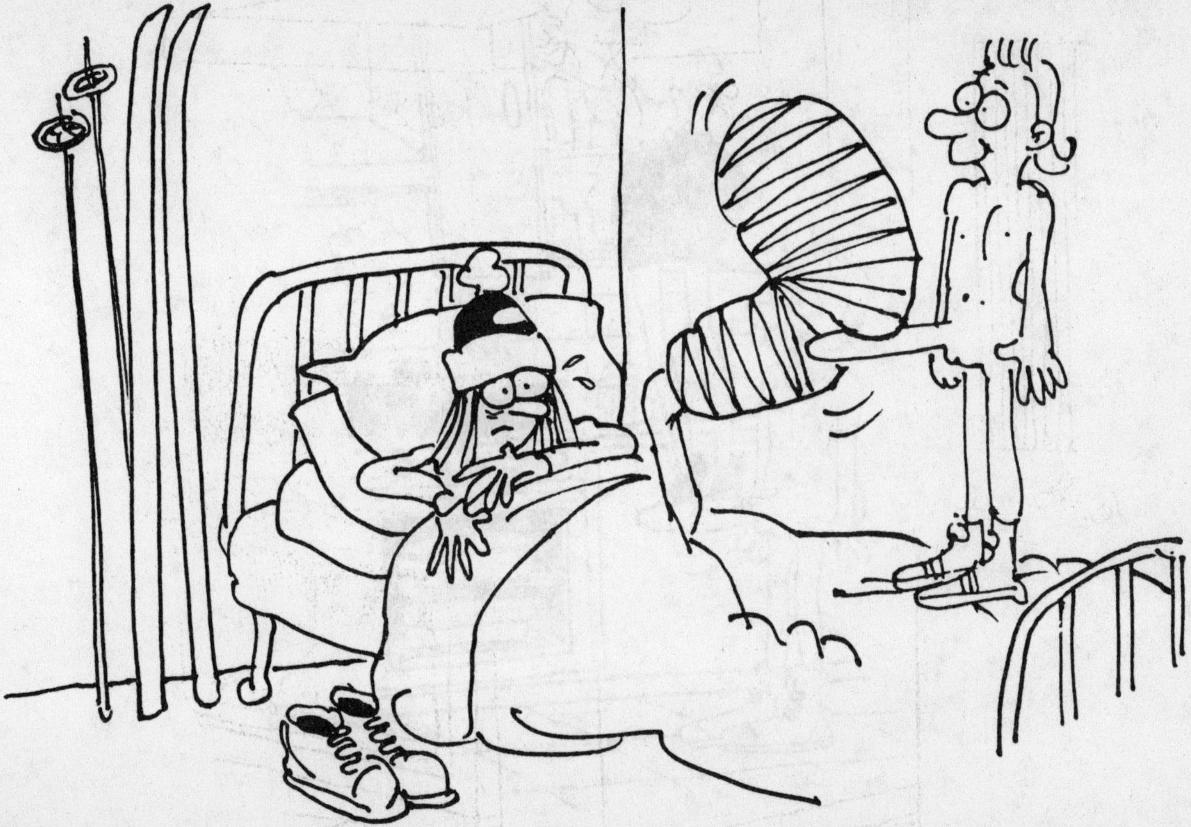

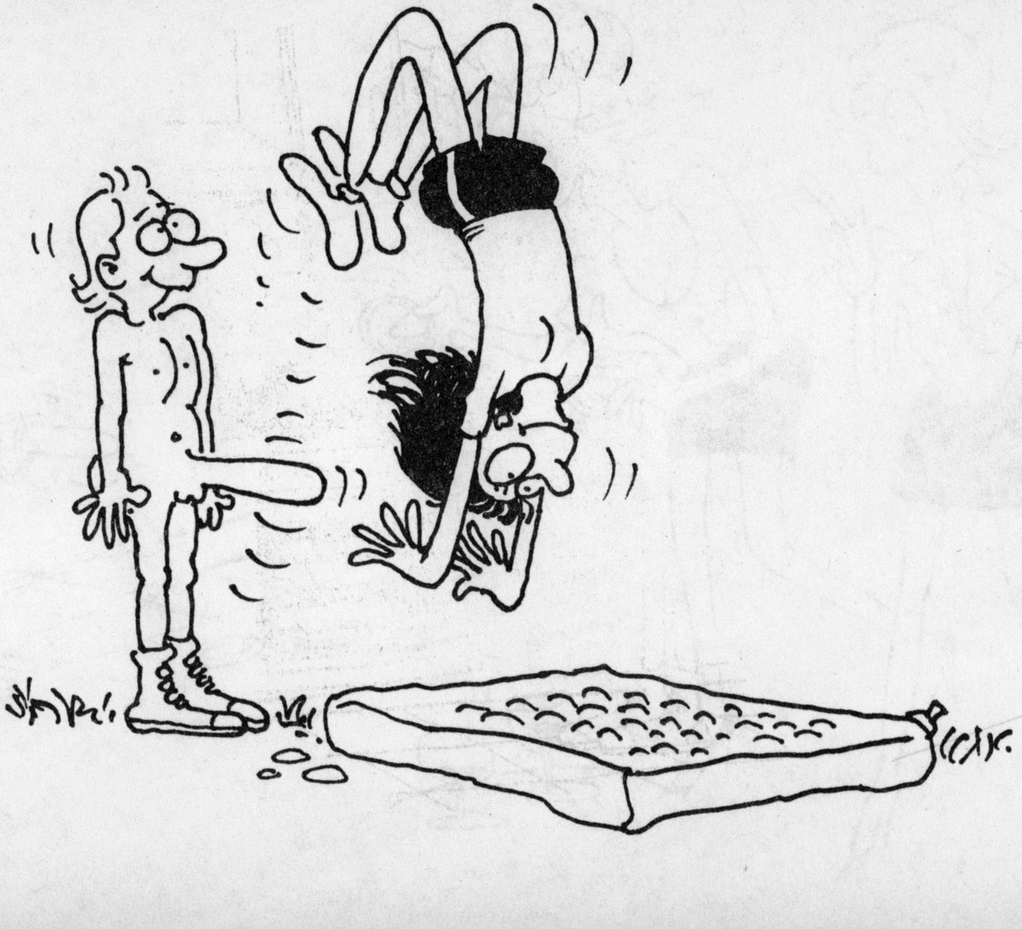

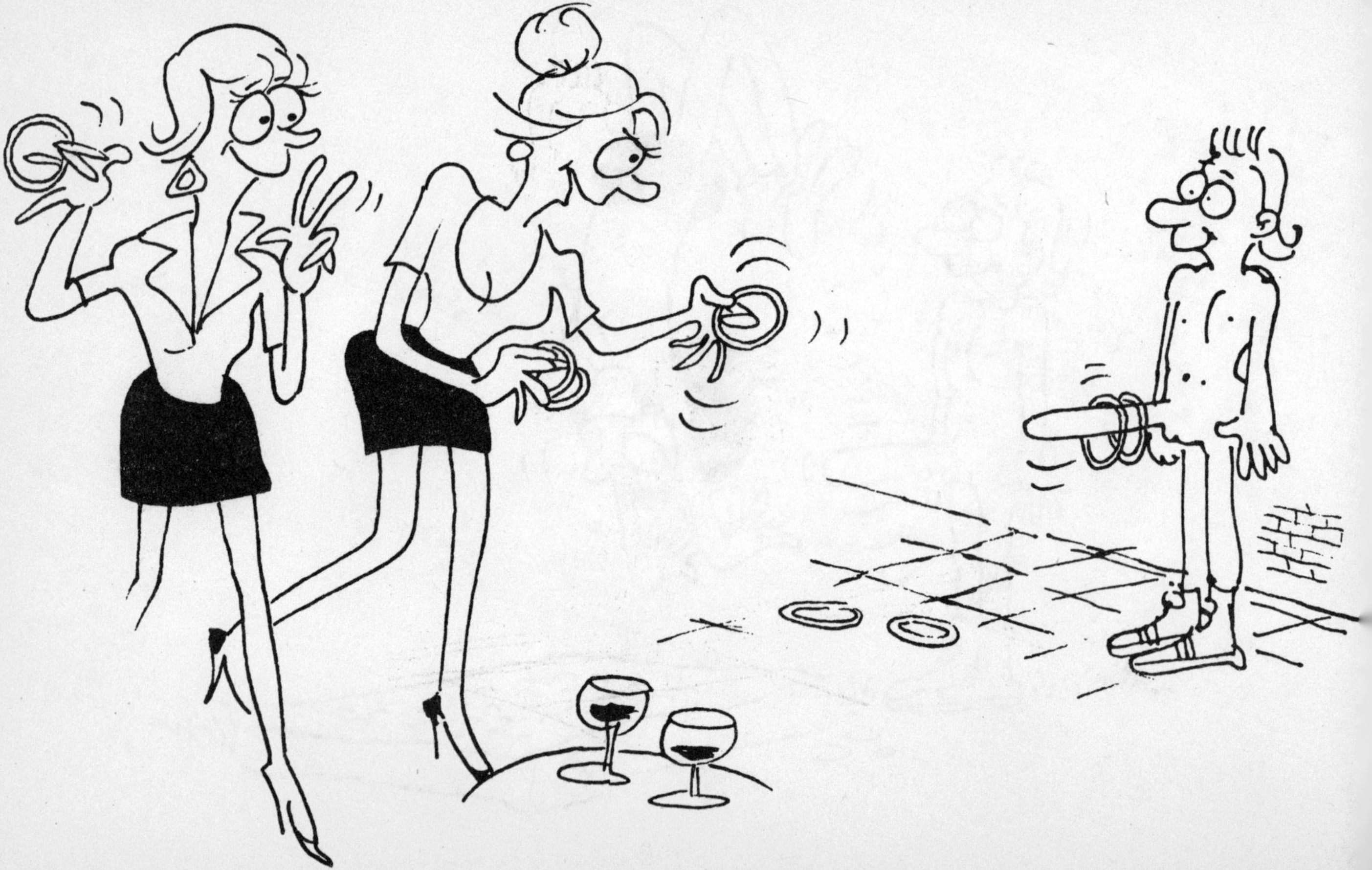

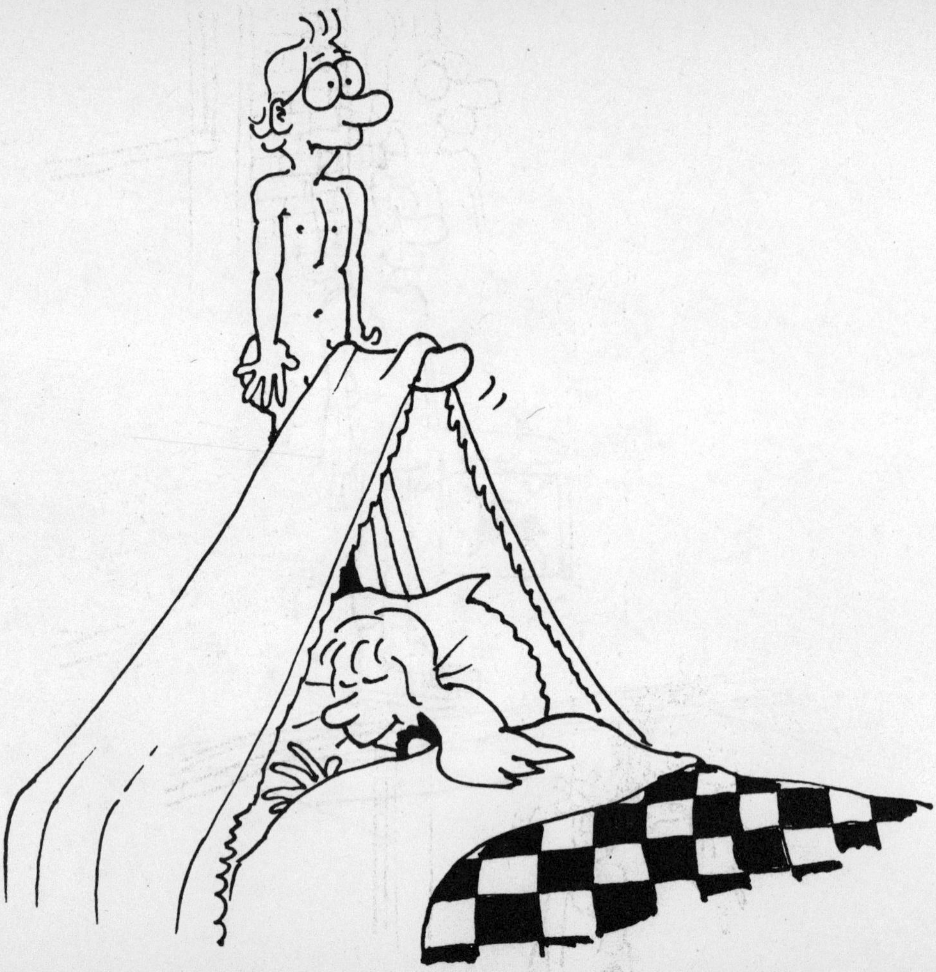

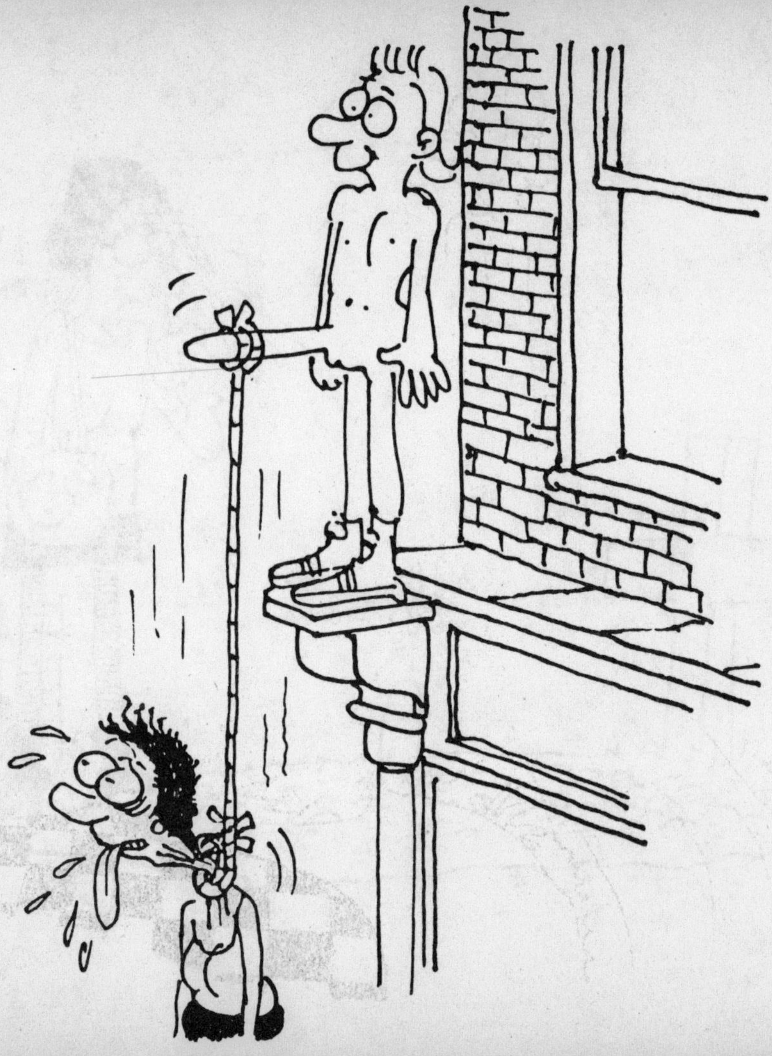

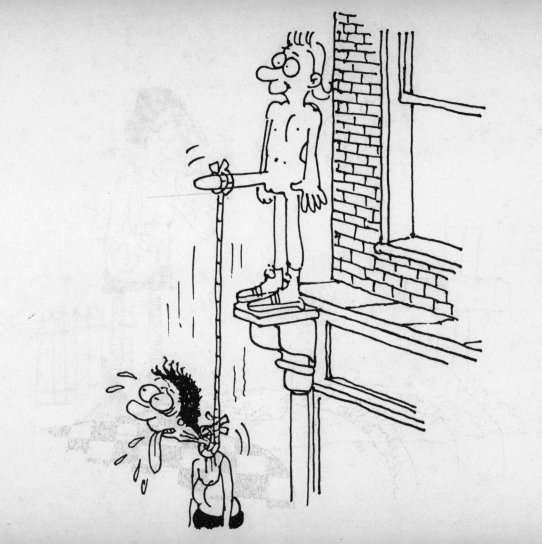